GLISTENING GOLDEN CIRCLE

Volume 1

Publications by Lorenza Palomino

King of Innocence and Peace: *The Guiltlessness In You: A Poetic Truth*

Forgiveness Is the Key: *You Are the Key, a Poetic Truth*

Godzillion Worlds *A poetic collection of universes that exist beyond us*

Other works appear in:

The Golden Letter Of Memory *in #1 Capsized: The Pandemic Lockdown (Summer Seasonal 2020)*

Review of The Golden Letter Of Memory, Lockdown Perspective & Q&A Interview *in #2 The Fall And Rise Of Chimeras (Autumn Seasonal 2020)*

Righteous True Meaning *in Volume 1 - Gray: We Hide Our Colors Within (Anthology Volume Collection)*

GLISTENING GOLDEN CIRCLE

Volume 1

Lorenza Palomino

An Ink Gladiators Press® Publication

Ink Gladiators Press®
Publishing and promoting warriors on life's battlefield

Ink Gladiators Press® is an ePublishing company whose mission is to publish and promote writers, poets, lyricists, artists and photographers through our current worldwide market distribution of over 3 billion readership. It is not affiliated with any other organization and is an independent ePublishing house. For Earthians who want to publish with us, check out our ongoing publishing opportunities at Our Earthians Community Group, or write to us to learn more about our Celestial Sky Services at our email address: contact@inkgladiatorspress.com.

First Edition

Glistening Golden Circle - Volume 1
ISBN 13 - 978-81-949418-4-2

Ink Gladiators Press®
Bangalore, India
www.inkgladiatorspress.com

Credits:
Digital Painting, Cover & Book Design - Leonie Belle Hawk
Editor-in-Chief – Reena Doss

Dedications

To God the Almighty for permitting His Holy Spirit to teach and guide me through quantum leap.

To Jesus Christ, Lord, savior and brother. Thank you for draping the cape of royalty and peace over my shoulders during difficult times.

To my eternal holy friend, the Holy Spirit, I am ever so honored to work alongside of you.

To my lovely friend and mentor, Irene Peralez, I am grateful for your divine ethereal guidance during the years I knew nothing of celestial righteousness. I value and cherish your friendship forevermore.

To humanity and all life forms on earth, throughout the whole wide universe, its galactic societies and dimensions, I hope you read this book one day in love, joy and peace.

Table Of Contents

Foreword

Lorenza Palomino is undoubtedly a controversial spiritual writer of today's modern network of visionists because you are never quite sure if she exists in the past, present or future realm of this universe.

Having worked with her closely over the last year, I discovered that her raw manuscripts consist of a child-like style of viewing the world yet there is also a deep maturity of wisdom gained from her personal experiences with God throughout her life. Her previous two books: *Forgiveness Is The Key: You Are The Key, A Poetic Truth* and *King of Innocence and Peace: The Guiltlessness In You: A Poetic Truth* provide new perspectives into the process of spiritual growth and understanding one's purpose in the midst of chaos. With touching vulnerability, she will take you through her own struggles of loss, grief, self-discovery, forgiveness and repentance as she finds her salvation in the release of sufferings in the miraculous cross of Christ.

When I began reading her Glistening Golden Circle series, I was intrigued on realizing how different the content was from her previous books. Here, she focuses more on prayerful dedications, poetic reflections and essays of intrinsic digging into the supernatural way of things. As this is the first volume in the trilogy, I recommend looking at it with fresh eyes so you can notice how each piece links to the main theme of hope in the eternal life when this world passes away.

I met Lorenza Palomino about a month after I launched Ink Gladiators Press in 2020 so I was quite excited to welcome her aboard my growing network of authors. Over a period of 13 months, I began to understand her on a deeper level and found myself drawn to her generosity of spirit, kindness of heart and patience of the soul. Her complete faith and trust in my team's ability to do our best for her book babies was so humbling.

Her gentleness and professionalism in handling unexpected delays and obstacles during this difficult time of Covid-19 is something I will always remember her for.

To summarize, Lorenza is someone who will chuckle at life's downs and raise you up when you feel low. She will look for every reason to understand when things are not what she is used to and she has the most fascinating way of letting go of what she cannot control by surrendering herself to the inevitable. Even though we do not share the same belief systems, my personal interactions with her have always been one of respect, dialogue and non-judgment. We enjoy varied conversations as we mutually appreciate each other and yet acknowledge our differences without worrying about conflict.

Glistening Golden Circle - Volume 1 is an invitation to explore concepts of belief, spirituality and religion while simultaneously appreciating different points of views and teaching oneself how to grow exponentially in mind, body and spirit when you see with eyes of faith.

God bless you all!

Reena Doss @reenadossauthor
CEO & Founder | Ink Gladiators Press®
www.inkgladiatorspress.com

Preface

"The unforgiving mind is a downfall
but the forgiving mind is a divine call."

There are many on earth and throughout the universe that are very much aware that the experiences all life forms endure through illusional life encounters as we traverse through earth and other worlds in universes and dimensions are all an act. During the duration of time, there are poetic rollercoaster rides we take through dream worlds to come out of the other side into the Kingdom of realism. The ultimate ethereal spiritualists to learn of spirituality is through the Trinity. This is where we learn and remember everything we wish to behold and know untangling what is fabricated and what is factual. If Christ Himself emerged from the heaven's and told you this, would you believe it?

This book takes you deeper into spirituality and introduces you to things most of us on earth do not think of. The choice is yours to take it for what it's worth and permit yourself to spiritually grow in ways you never thought possible. To deny it is to stay trapped in illusion. The goal is to help you rise through forgiveness to enter the glisten circle of hope where spiritual experiences of faith awaits your willingness to behold and know all that your heart desires.

There is regularly a deep hymn of music relentlessly going on throughout the universe inside. When we permit forgiveness to enter our life with the gift of divine healing of thought pattern is when we allow ourselves to hear Heaven's harps.

At the instant you hear the elegance of Heaven's music, forgiveness enters with such tender ease. She is a blessing on a grandeur level! When you receive her without wrestle, you most certainly cannot fail. The unforgiving mind is a downfall, the forgiving mind is such a divine up call.

Cherish and value forgiveness dearly, for she permits you to behold the glistening circle of hope inside ever so sweetly, swiftly and in all clarity and certainty. This is an important dive into spiritual experiences of faith where you meet the golden glisten of love, light, life and truth of everything!

Introduction

"Do not give up in righteousness, persevere through your willingness to transform with the Holy Spirit and you undoubtedly prevail."

I strongly, but humbly and divinely encourage you to read this poetic truth with an open mind and heart, for all the prewritten and predestined events are inescapable. But, they can be altered as oneself remembers the glistening circle of hope, a quantum leap into spiritual experiences of faith where spirit recalls what is fabricated and what is factual.

The ego will try to detour you into its web of devilish thinking, which are negative thoughts from the perspective of a horizontal axis. Remember not to allow yourself to fall into its sticky web of merciless temptations only to be trapped in it and remain imprisoned in its brutal and false world. It will always lead you to dead end roads full of curves and swerves only to confuse you as to where you must go, leading you to feel you are alone and unloved.

Be willing not to permit it to bring you to walls you keep bumping into time and time again that lead you to feel you are going crazy in its maze of lies of wretchedness, confusion, guilt and shame. The ego structures are holographic images that diffract you in chaotic ways. Because its primary goal is to redirect you away from the glistening circle of hope, even though it does not know it is there. However, it can sense that you are attempting to leave its crazy sinister prison. This is why when you are attempting to get right it seems everything goes wrong. Persevere in righteousness. Through willingness you undoubtedly prevail.

Remember, God cannot fail and neither can you. Be willing to stick to Christ Atonement like glistening golden glue of dew because deep down inside, you really do not want to take a ruthless, senseless, meaningless and hellish ride. The glistening golden circle inside helps you uphold your divine love, joy and peace. The Holy Spirit awaits your calling in patience and in peace. Be willing to listen to His soft peaceful Voice in you and embrace His lead. He leads to the sparkly golden road of Heaven where there are no walls to run into and no curves to swerve through.

God's golden road of eternity tenderly completes the axis of upside down thinking to right side up thinking. This is where you can be honored with the crown of knowledge in time.

Prologue

"Dreamer born from out of a far-away Kingdom
where only the spirit can withstand its silent freedom,
where one day again, you hold my hand."

It always begins with dreamy-like-worlds that are physically born into the universe's kingdom where the ancient phases of the past, present and future commenced godzillions ago. My palms sweat, my heart pounds and my tummy rolls thinking about how everything that was made enters every phase of its dreamy unfolding.

It is natural to cheerfully hold hands in the deepest adoration and admiration of ethereal and cerebral connection. All have gone away from a far-away Kingdom to be born into a land that can physically withstand sweet pleasures where bitter episodes inevitably unfold. When they do unravel, it is only because it is the day and hour every dreamer appointed it to enter. Before everyone was born, we wrote our life script right alongside one another and which brought every soul into agreement. Every dreamer spiraled into the debts of the universe's kingdom to artificially be born out of a womb—that houses the embryo—into dream worlds.

In the realm of the physical, eventually, the mind spirals, trying to understand how illusional kingdoms came into existence. To be born in such merciless forms feels so real but deep down inside the dreamer's own universe is where one knows there is a better kingdom from which existence must come from. However, it takes courage to dive into the glistening circle of hope where, instinctively, the dreamer knows there has got to be an excursion into spiritual experiences of faith.

The day one decides to take the leap is where the mind discovers a Kingdom that is sweet but first, there is a dimension that the dreamer must get past in order to behold the celestial Kingdom from which everyone comes from. The dreamer must get past the tangled maze of hellish illusions and the celestial ride into quantum leap, undoubtedly, untangles what is fabricated and what is factual.

Does the dreamer embrace the ride to rise beyond what has been told through dreams or does the dreamer remain planted in the world's view of illusion?

Baby Juliana

(Dedicated to baby Juliana, born from Heaven to Earth
on September 25, 2016; Virginia, Earth.)

Baby Juliana born in September,
a holy day of celebration in the state of Virginia, Earth.

Baby Juliana born in September,
always remember you come from Heaven
and your birth into the world
brings a jewel of a smile
to dada, mama and also, nana.

Baby Juliana born in Virginia,
always remember the sanctified day of September,
for you are a divine blessing,
never ceasing to bring cheerful, tearful delight
to the hearts of many.

Baby Juliana born in September,
remember your part in creating
all that you see through physical eyes.
The day arrives when you will behold
the Kingdom of Heaven through the eyes of the Holy Spirit.
He inevitably guides you through this dream world
to the golden road of Heaven
where you will behold the true from the false.

When this happens, it is because your time
has entered into the remembrance
of the invisible Kingdom that you will return to.

In all clarity and certainty,
this can only happen through spiritual vision,
a quantum leap into your divine mission.

Your part in making Earth
before you were even born gives you the right
to freely spree every part of it for it is your birthright.
Just ask the Holy Spirit and He helps you remember
the truth of the free spirit in you
as co-creator with God and your brethren.

Baby Juliana, always remember
the tender love and light of Jesus Christ,
for He smiles upon your hallowed birth of temporal life.

Never forget His love and light is no curse.
He is the only one who never forsakes
because He loves you
and will always be with you everywhere you go.

Baby Juliana, remember that one day,
you will recognize the atonement of Christ
He offers you every day of your life, twenty-four seven.
It is when you are willing to receive
that Jesus Christ enters to reconcile
His love and light with your own,
for He is your brother in Heaven
where you are truly free to spree as a spirit
in the realm of divinity and eternity!

His free spirit is one with you,
meaning, you are never alone.

Part 1
Glistening Roads

Earth's forgiven wanderers and dreamers witness and experience bittersweet episodes of their prewritten life script.

The Worst Or The Best

In a world of corruption, we think
the worst that can happen is death.

In reality, death is
a transformation and transition
from this kingdom of corruption
to the Kingdom of beautification.

The transformation
is a quantum leap process.
It is a transformation
from mortality to immortality
where the spirit is released
from the imprisonment of the body.
This is where it transitions
into eternal bliss.

This is a blessing
if you pre-elected to lovingly caress
the loveliness inside
while you still have the chance
to do so in the illusion
of self-destruction and self-deceit.

There is nothing
more beautiful than the liberty
from mortality to immortality
or when we transition
into the Kingdom of Heaven
we have been gone from
since godzillions ago.

In worlds of illusion,
the worst that can happen
is fighting against what is inevitable.
This is where
we prolong our suffering.

The best that can happen
is surrender to the Holy Ghost
by letting oneself go
when the time arrives
for you to go home.

The end of the illusional life
in our profound suffering
is our calling, our time
to return home.
Yet we fight it
rather than embrace it.

We prolong this calling
because we do not remember
the eternal beauty of the Kingdom
we already belong to.

In terminal suffering,
it is okay to let the desire of oneself
be released from a world of gloom.

Rejoice in such a glorious feat,
for when the time arrives
to set the spirit free,
let it peacefully be.

God calls us home
when the worst has passed away.
Yet, the best is yet to come
when we rise into Heaven's Kingdom.

Let the spirit rise in a glisten
golden light of glory!

Why stay in the Kingdom we do not belong
when God is calling us back home?
What do you want—
the worst or the best?

Merciless Temptation

Born into a merciless world
where it is destined to worship
a premade ruthless father
to love and worship
while it sustains itself in us
where the mind and heart abide.

With every stride taken
we are blind to the divine fact
instilled inside.
We can only behold and know
that through our willingness
to rise
from the ego's cruel world
of fear and darkness
is a quantum leap
toward the journey of divinity
out of the fog
of its clogged and bleak thinking
where you will find yourself
sinking into the abyss
of its madness.

Here, we are callously selfish
and greedy, for we do not care
about the survival
of all those who are
selflessly needy.

We trespass ruthlessly
because we think
we are deserving of it.
But this is self-deceiving
for what we are doing is
conserving merciless temptation
of sick thinking
into isolation and desolation.

At your willingness
holiness enters to help
unravel all confusion, guilt and shame
of self-deception and self-destruction.
The devoutness inside,
inevitably rises
bringing union to communion.

It's like peeling layers of an onion
as you tear your way to its core
to get the juicy part of its tasty savory.
It's the same journey
as we get through merciless temptation
to finally reach
divine attraction into unity.

You behold, know, receive and admit
in all clarity and certainty
without feeling confused, shame and guilt
about anything divinity offers
because the core of godliness within
purifies all sin.

This is where you no longer tear up
over the peeling of an onion
because divinity is the essence
into the depths of love, light, life and truth
where you become a witness
to the tears of anguish
as they disappear into nothingness.

For the Holy Spirit
wipes the slate clean
at your willingness
to save the day
from the merciless temptation
of your own sick thinking.

You learn to return
to miracle mindedness
just as Christ did,
full of the clergy of God's mercy
where you become a savior
to your brothers' comfort and contentment
and to your own.

We have reached the era to end
greediness, homelessness, starvation,
stealing, killing, thieving and grieving.

This is all accomplished
by your willingness to toss
merciless temptation
to return to miracle thinking
where you no longer are sinking
into the wrathful father's puny kingdom
of a thoughtless, sightless and heartless demeanor
that is creepy and wickedly deceiving.

Remember this when you are witness
to its annoying loud mouth,
so wide open
you cannot even see
its devious or adorable face
that inevitably cast itself into oblivion.

Where we were once callous,
we are now caring.
Where we were once ruthless,
we are now righteous.
Where we were once selfish,
we are now selfless.
Where we were once greedy,
we are now princely.

We smile sweetly ablaze
happy to assist a brother's survival
without expecting them
to return the favor.

We have learned to give
from the divine part of the mind and heart
and it is here where we dodge bitter dart tragedies
because we are too busy
collecting God's blessings.

Every time we bow to collect
the bitter dart gifts of calamity,
it misses its target.
This is a quantum leap
from the release out of the bittersweet world
of merciless temptation
where you are free
to be your brother's salvation.

Return to miracle thinking
and rise from merciless temptation
that the ego tries to spear you to.

The divine power invested in you
is greater than
the puny, ruthless, loud mouth god
callously ruling all dream worlds
throughout the whole universe.

It is through
faith, atonement and forgiveness
that we triumph
when we take a quantum leap
from the realm of complexity
into the wonderment of simplicity.

Accountability

We turn away from the holiness of forgiveness
in our time of bereavement to ensure we hold one another
accountable to horrid episodes.

Let us remember
that forgiveness is plentiful
in the midst of
heartbreaking episodes.
To behold
what is beyond the physical
is to see the holiness
in you and me,
which is utterly remarkable.

This is possible
through our willingness
to align our mind with God's
to undoubtedly find
what it is we are looking for.
Isn't love, joy, peace and freedom
all that we seek?

Through readiness,
He gently slips
into the alignment of our thoughts
where we connect the dots.

This brings a holy connection
where we behold
the gem of forgiveness
in the midst of contentious.

Calmness and peacefulness prevails
when we clearly behold
the holiness and sinlessness
within all of us.

Let time take its place
where the healing and correction
of every mistake is
only temporarily displaced.

Through forgiveness,
Holiness and sinlessness prevails
and all mistakes
are tenderly healed and corrected.

Accountability is banished
because God's love, joy, peace and freedom
are forever reestablished.

Forget What Was

We spend a lifetime thriving
on what was.

Murdered people are remembered,
a reminder of the killers
and the devastating tragedy
the victims endured.

We think
the murdered ones are dead.
The truth is
they are more alive than we are
because a killer can destroy
the body
but they cannot touch
the spirit.

It is better not to thrive
on the murdered ones
because no one
can take your life.

Rejoice in the release of spirit
who finally returns to Heaven
because where they go
is a much better Kingdom
where they await
your return home.
They are freed from prison,
released from
the world of pains and sorrows.

They have utilized their time
and finished their life's mission scripts.
The way in which we are released
is the way we have chosen
to leave this world.

They are now
in the Kingdom of Heaven
where there is no more suffering
like in this senseless dream world
of fears and tears.

Forgive the killers
and uphold their salvation and your own.
Be lifted in love, joy and peace
where you will begin to see
that there is no such thing
as the deceased.

Embrace the release of the spirit
who is called to its home
in a state of grace
and is no longer
displaced.

The Kingdom of Heaven is so glorious
that we forget what was
yet never was.

Passing Through

My feet walk
the grounds of this earth,
but still I feel as if I do not belong
where I traverse.

Its gravity is too heavy
for me to bear
yet I know salvation is near.
I look beyond the sky
to behold the constellations
of universes' nations.

I recall
that I am just passing through
this world of illusion
where Hades is experienced
and mortality is a fatality.

Somehow I know, I will return
to the true reality
which is the essence of divinity—
a Kingdom of eternity
where immortality
is factuality in all its totality,
a realm of joviality
where silence and stillness abide
escaping the noise and craziness
of every egotistical thought
of dream-like-states that lure me
into its venomous traps.

A web of lies so mangled
my mind becomes entangled
not sure where to begin
to untangle the messy dreams of thought.

Then I reach for
His outstretched hand
and there, I unweave
the tangled web of self-deception
to journey into the path
of healing and correction.

Just like you,
I am passing through
the illusion of Hades and mortality.
We do inevitably find our way
to divinity, eternity and immortality.
The true nature of mentality
where wellness of mind abides.

I no longer divide,
I let holiness guide.
This is how I elect to escape
the hellish realms of humanities illusion
as I am passing through earth's gravity.

Travesty, I will escape
because my spirit lives and ascends
to the glory of the Kingdom of Heaven.

Miracle Thinking

Minds of insanity snake deeper downward
into the abyss of madness.

It is a deep seeded spiral of carnal thinking
that we keep sinking deeper into
the wrath of fear and darkness.

We must be willing to return
to miracle thinking to escape
the downward spiral
permitting it to reverse upward
to dance skyward
from out of the spiral of insanity
and into the grandiose of sanity.

Showers of blessings and happiness
wipes out all sadness on remembering
that miracle thinking raises us
from sinking deeper into insanity
releasing us from vanity.

At our willingness, we can do this
which is the ultimate escape
from the web of arrogance
and rise in humility
for the divine sake of humanity.

Miracle thinking is no casualty,
for it is drastically divine and naturally fashionable
to be made absolutely admirable and utterly adorable.
Miracle thinking is an incredible achievement
in a world that is out of order
drowning in hate.

But remember it is all fake,
so let's get with it
and embrace miracle thinking
in the willingness to meet each other's needs
which abolishes selfishness and greed;
a stepping stone where we behold
the stairway to Heaven.

Hitch a ride on the glistening golden white vine
spiraling heavenward illuminating
that dance of golden light
all happy to rise in delight
to take a flight from the fear of night.

There will be no need
to steal, kill, destroy, thieve and grieve
when we lovingly, caringly and selflessly
give everything freely
to meet the needs of humanity.

Miracle thinking does not send you sinking,
it is a blessing that ends ruthless trespassing.

Iron Fist

Born into a culture that rules
the household with an iron fist
puts a twist on one's desire to fly the nest
and be the best in their life where they wish to rest.

This brings chaos to families with an iron fists
who demand no forgiveness
and don't accept the wishes and desires
of those yearning to take the journey
toward their own learning.
They are accused of dishonor
and sadly murdered because they believe
that cruel feats like this
will restore family honor.
But no matter the passion
to restore family honor,
the killer runs and hides,
a dead giveaway, a demonstration—
knowing they have done wrong
and yet, they do not know
what they have done.
The killers remain in hiding
to ensure they are not captured,
shackled and labeled as guilty
as they are judged, convicted and imprisoned
for the murderous deed done
yet, murder is illusion.

Illusion or not,
we still must be willing to learn
to step out of darkness
of the controlling iron fist
and forgive and accept one's decision,
desires and wishes to fly the nest
to discover the best way
to live out their own life script.

Even though Christ tells us
what happens is because it was agreed upon.
As I mentioned before,
the life script can be changed
through our self-awareness
to not fall into wicked temptations
for there is no honor in the belief
to kill those who wish to do their will.
It is better not to force
or drill your own will upon another.
Let others spread their wings
to find their way to fulfill their dreams.
The belief to kill is a way
of blinding ourselves to the fabrication
of an iron fist script we can be free from.
The controlling iron fist
merely hurdles the mind deeper into madness.

The feats of the iron fist
is a sad and heartbreaking episode
that spears the hearts of humanity
of such senseless insanity.

My Stalker

In the beginning of the voyage of spiritual awakening
the timidness was hideous.

I was desperate and determined
to come out of my own ruthless dreams
of self-deception.
I was not brave enough to be saved
so I wandered through this world
in a merciless maze.
I shivered in my own skin
through every phase
of my awakened dreams.

He tenderly worked His miracles in me
to ensure that I rise
from the wooziness of dreams.
It took so long to master the test of faith
through the journey
of every disastrous phase of awakened dreams.
Even the episodes of my stalker's own dream
who would not leave me alone
felt like an obsessive horror flick
that goes on and on and on for way too long
dragged out for years.

During the occurrences of my stalker,
I was determined to prove to myself
that faith in God is all I need to ensure the prowler
would wake up from his dreary dream
where his mad mania gets washed away
down God's glistening golden stream of holy water,
renewing, healing and correcting
my stalker's sick thought pattern.

During this two year season of being stalked,
I was told to call the cops and have him chained,
shackled, arrested, judged, convicted and imprisoned
but I declined against this worldly bondage.

My friends were frustrated
when I elected not to incarcerate him.
I stood my ground and kept my grip of faith in God
knowing that He would certainly deliver
and redeem him from his fixation
of the ego's sick flirtation.
Faith is what I had to prove to myself
that *she* is with us no matter how long it takes
to wash away my stalker's obsession
and into the bliss of freedom
from such a ridiculous mess of our life scripts.
Every day I went about my business,
not giving any attention to his sickness,
trying to tame the queasiness in my own tummy.
Rather, I lifted him up in prayer
and took his nauseating obsession
and laid it upon God's golden feet at the golden altar
of forgiveness and redemption from this sick dream
we both agreed upon before we were even born.
No matter the frustration,
I asked that my stalker be delivered
from the fixation of the devil's dictation
and let the sickness rise from his mind
into the flotation of the airflow
where it poofs like vapor
into the mist of the sun
into the nothingness it truly is.
Until the day that this happened!
In my heart of hearts,
I knew that faith would come through
no matter how long it took.

I thank God for holding me up
during the times I no longer wished
to overlook my stalker's engrossment
and instead, have him booked.
It took two years for this awakened dream
to shatter into oblivion.
We did it without chains, shackles, judgment,
conviction, imprisonment, bloodshed and tears
because through the divine power invested in me,
I was able to let my stalker remain free
when I permitted myself to endure to the end
to ensure I passed the test of faith
so we both get released
from this horrid dream of insanity.

When my stalker awakened from his possession,
there was no question to the deliverance
he gained from his own obsession.
My perseverance in faith enabled Him
to release us into the divinity of freedom,
love, joy and peace and into redemption
simultaneously and harmoniously.

I behold through the sovereignty of divinity
invested in us, the Kingdom of spirituality
where it is all gloriously worthy to endure
every dreadful episode through love, faith, kindness,
humbleness, forgiveness, peace,
patience, perseverance and consistency.

*We are witnesses to God's miraculous love, light
and tender healing, correction and redemption
through every insane occurrence that screams out
for swift divine intervention simultaneously and harmoniously.*

Monster

The term monster is used everywhere
to describe the heinous things
we bring one to another.

Dreams shatter through bogus murders
all over the universe.
When eyes open wide
to how hideous the worship of murder is,
we will get tired out, hearing day after day
all about this dreamy nonsense.

Learning the difference between
what is fabricated and what is factual
about these horrid events on ancient worlds,
boredom enters because the mind and heart
desires something much greater.

When all the bad news gets more and more frightful,
we remember to call each other monsters.
What we witness and experience now is nothing
when compared to what is to come.

We roam the surface of earth's soil
finding dreadful brutality or we dig up
vicious ancient things we believe are evidence
to the embodiment of heartless encounters.
We fear it because we do not have the remembrance of it.
The monster is frightful because we do not
look at it within our own psyche.

The monster lives in all of us
but so does holiness.
Holiness waits in patience and peace
for our willingness to heed to its righteous calling.

The evidence that the monster lives
inside—is in plain sight.
When we chain, shackle, judge,
convict and cage murderers or protesters,
we demonstrate the savage within.
This is the evidence of sameness inside
giving the monster the support it needs
to flourish in its merciless ways.
It is always a choice to listen
to the loud, puny voice of the monster
or the peaceful, righteous voice of holiness.
What we choose to listen to is what we nourish;
this is how we manifest it and it undoubtedly flourishes.
Through retaliation, we imprison the monster.
Through forgiveness, we redeem the monster.
Incarceration helps the monster grow
in higher monstrous ways.
Redemption helps the monster replenish
and flourish in godly ways.
Feed the monster righteousness
and we listen to the voice of holiness
which leads every mind and heart
to the threshold of forgiveness
where love, joy and peace flourish;
seeking those willing to embellish in holiness.

Listen to the loud distorted voice
and we feed the ego.
Listen to the soft, peaceful voice
and we let righteous enter
to redeem monster to the epitome of holiness
in the center of one's mind, heart and soul.

The ego is the monster
and the Holy Spirit is the righteous.

The Killer Who Let Me Go

His blindness fails to see
that my happiness is a front;
I felt that if I acted happy,
then perhaps it will ease my misery.

He picked me out because my cheerfulness
angered and annoyed him
when his own misery infuriated him.
He is angry and swiftly fading,
for he does not yet know
that giving into this form of temptation
spirals him deeper into its persuasion.
This only brings sadness to all parties connected
because there is short-lived happiness
in this world of evilness.
He was like a boa constrictor ready
to corral the strength of his muscle around me,
only to squeeze the life out of me.
In the grasp of his craziness,
I showed no fear and refused to shed a tear.
He was puzzled that I was not bedazzled,
but this was only another front
to hopefully sum up courage.

I gaze into his eyes and said,
"Do not judge a book by its cover,
for you do not know the mind and heart of another."
He glares at me.
I see a faint spark in his eye as if the light in him wishes to rise.
His glare softens and transforms to sorrow
as if he is about to cry.
He takes me by the hand and says,
"Let's go..."

I remain silent, hoping
he would lay down the violence.
In the midst of the night,
he drives me to a deserted dusty road
and orders me to get out!
He did not have to demand me twice!
With no hesitation,
I bolted away in fascination.

As he drives away down the dusty road,
I can only hope and pray
he would not stay in the continuation
of giving into this form of temptation.
I forgive the killer who let me go
because even in the clutches of his madness,
I forgave its evilness.
In the phase of the foolishness of his maze,
I saw his holy innocence and desire
to reign in love, joy and peace.
Through forgiveness,
the chains and shackles of bondage
broke and delivered us from evil.
I pray he drives into the light of goodness
to cleanse and purify all his madness.
In that moment of holiness, he heeded the calling
to let go of his ridiculous brawling.
The killer who let me go remains free
to find his way out of his universe of misery.
I lifted him up in prayer
so he settles in love, joy and peace,
for even he is deserving of release from the chains and
shackles
of the ego's sinister prison that has always been loosened.

He is just as much God's son
as you and I are.

Love Everyone and Everything

Through distorted thinking we fear and hate or do not like
worlds and figures no matter what form they take.

In dreams, we pass judgment
upon everyone and everything.
For everyone and everything
we fear, hate, dislike and complain about
or even make fun of
is what we ourselves become.
It is always pleasing to consume
our thoughts with the glory of light,
for it is here that we learn to love
everyone and everything we fear
dislike, hate, complain and make fun of.

Love is where the light enters.

It becomes easier to learn
of the innocence in everyone and everything.
In illusion, everyone and everything
are designs to act out what we are not.
To exhaust our thoughts
in the dreary fearsome circle
housing fear and hate causes one to faint.
To lay all negative forces at God's golden feet
is to enable your eyes to be witness
to the transformation
from corruption to honesty,
the true reality
inside everyone and everything.
This is the ultimate way
to consume ourselves in love,
then everyone and everything becomes love.

Under the light of divinity,
the power of love combined
shines upon it.
This makes room for God
to show us how we can
humbly, kindly, patiently and peacefully
defeat the things we fear and hate
without ever having to faint.
Under the veil of mercy and grace,
we clearly behold and know
darkness has no power over us
unless we give our divine sovereignty to it
by cowering it through fear and hate.
Love tenderly overpowers
because it empowers everyone and everything
fearful and hateful to beautiful and delightful,
for this is what's at the core of everyone and everything
we fear and hate.
Through God's mercy and grace
is where we get past the maze of fear and hate,
the foolish thinking through ego's eye.
In the end, love and light
is what we find at the center of every reality.
This is the case at the base
of every frightful feature and figure.
Rise from bereavement into the wonderment of love and light
enabling eyes to clearly behold how heartless it truly is
to fear, hate, dislike, make fun of and complain.

This is where we gain spiritual vision and knowledge
where we look past flesh and bones and behold the heart of gold
when we love everyone and everything.

Glistening Circle of Hope

For a time, we have forgotten
that God gives but never takes.

He is the purity of divine gold,
glistening tenderly bold in everyone and everything
For He is your creator that built His divine creations
around His love and light no matter its form.

For one day, you behold all the divinity
in everyone and everything.
This enables you to assist the Holy Spirit
to share God's word of love, light, life and truth
to ensure that everyone and everything
are found and led to divinity.

To be born into worlds of illusion
is the dreary bubble of synthetic pleasures,
frights, pains and sorrows.
At our own willingness,
we left the glistening circle of hope,
the Kingdom of timelessness.

Yet, its radiance in all its glory of authenticity
is where we left behind all the enjoyable moments
and treasures that await our return home in the faith of hope.

The physical forms in synthetic worlds
upholds deep within the mind the golden altar.
When everyone and everything are willing to reach it
by looking past flesh and bones,
we behold the glistening circle of hope.

The glistening golden circle is embedded with God's love,
light, life and truth, the essence of what He, Heaven and Self
(spirit) is
and to allow yourself to hear His Voice
is absolutely your choice.

Let your mind define in all clarity and certainty
what the glistening circle of hope houses,
for beyond the clouds of darkness,
we all go home in divine alertness
and as the old saying goes,
Only God knows.

Holiness, sinlessness, wholeness, wholesomeness, kindness,
humbleness, peacefulness, guiltlessness, compassion, joy,
freedom, unity, safety, generosity, immortality and royalty
are the divine qualities of the glistening circle of hope
and it has always been.

At your willingness to learn to remember the divinity inside,
it will enable you to embrace and behold
all the divine qualities the glistening circle of hope offers.

God never takes away
what He has already given at creation.

Heaven's Embrace

At Heaven's embrace, maintain a straight face
as you witness no rat race or any form of disgrace.

The openness of Heaven is inviting,
behold it as an eyewitness
through the open arms of Christ,
who wraps His embracement,
the threshold of His enthronement.

His glistening golden love flows
through the tender sovereignty
of His ocean blue eyes
smiling ablaze as you gaze in amazement,
all too happy to encase Him.
Gliding beyond the spiritual staircase
leads to Heaven's encirclement,
now face to face, arms interlace,
heart to heart
with the glistening golden Christ.

Heaven's embrace is welcoming,
never again you feel unloved and out of place.
His welcome is a holy herb of grace
where you are an open light of energy,
free to be everywhere.

Heaven's embrace, your birthplace where
your light joins. It is neat to be free to
be. Your light outshines the vast darkness of
the universe free to spiritually traverse.

Heaven's embrace is no hiding place,
its openness is a holy welcome
of your return to the Kingdom.

A world you interlace
like the glistening golden white vine
lovingly forever intertwined
where there is no such thing as time.

Heaven's embrace,
your birthplace where logic is wholesome;
A neurologic state of mind
where you never think twice.
There is no guessing,
just simply knowing.

Come, be free to your true identity.

Grace Most Amazing

Interlace with grace most amazing.
she is a gift from the holy Kingdom.

She will not steer you wrong,
for she can only lead you
to the golden road of Heaven.

Heed to God's blessings
remembering everything experienced
are simple lessons to learn by.

Gaze upon her glorious face
and let the brilliance of her light rays
shine upon all your illusional days.

Embrace the loveliness of grace
and she leads to the pearly gates
of the Kingdom of Heaven.

She is such a lovely gift God freely gives
so merciful and true
she takes away all illusional blues.

She is a blessing that saves you
from optical illusion,
for she offers spiritual sight to behold
where you once were blind but now you see.
She gives you ears to hear
where you once were deaf
but now you hear
the sweet hymns of her calling.

Her tender and sweet hymn
is most delightful in all her devout ways.

She is the sugar that frees you
from all deceitful slays
and into the splendor of godly ways.

She is the prodigy of God's sovereignty,
a gift of His blessings of mercy
leading you to God's holy clergy
of His grace most amazing.

Grace most amazing, how sweet her name.

Bring Me Out of the Illusion

O, how I feel most clogged
in the mist of illusional fog.

I clench my fist and try to settle
but I walk upon sharpened pebbles.

I twirl my hair with a nervous flare.
I do my best to bear, but I no longer care.
Let me not zone into an android glare.

O Father, I am in dire need of prayer.
The silent cry of my screams
brings me into a state of dreams.
I am extremely bored!
Bring me out of illusions,
full of tainted brutalization.
As I roam beneath your feet,
hear my pleas, for I am in urgent need
to be lifted up from this boredom.

You hand me a rose without thorns
but, the only thing I can think
is where to go
as a tear slowly flows down my cheek
only to land on the petal
of the rose I keep.

O, give me strength to live the full length,
bring me some goodness
in this dream of foolish boredom.
Stretch out your hand
where I can softly land
in the bosom of your embrace
of mercy and grace.

O how I behold my spirit
intertwined in a world I do not belong.
Let me wind down to safeguard
my mind of boredom.
Far too often, I am homesick;
let me go home so I no longer
need to roam in misery of sickly boredom!
Upon the crown of my head,
sprinkle gold and silver,
let it twinkle in the glimmer
of mind and spirit to bring me out
of the illusion where I do not belong.
I have been gone from Heaven for way too long.

Let me intertwine into your clasp,
the warm welcome of your tender grasp.
Like a soft cushion of the heart
where I no longer taste the tart of illusion,
I have atoned and now wish to go home.
Bring me out of the ancient illusion,
for it is so boring after atoning.

I am now ready to be with you
in the holiness of your presence
in the Kingdom of Heaven.
Bring me out of the ancient illusion,
let me transform from body to spirit.
Let me transition
out of the dream of bored bereavement
and ascend into the bliss
of the openness of Heaven's elegance.

I now behold clearly
what this glorious achievement brings.

Release Me

Let me no longer cling to the things of the world,
for it is a dream I wish to wake from
even if I think I want to remain asleep.

Let me no longer waste my life
to the dictations of the devil.
For it is senseless, meaningless and evil
to stay shackled in the dream world
of the ego's sinister prison.

Release me from the dream
I no longer wish to deem,
for everything is never what it seems.
Release me from any and all confusion
of the world of illusion,
for it is now too tiny for me to bear.
Now that I see in all clarity and certainty,
I am unsuitable of such senseless mind games
that thrive on fear and darkness.
I am royalty, please bring me back to the loyalty
I always had for you.

O Father in Heaven,
let this be my haven.

Release me from the world of fear and darkness
and let me cling to the bosom
of your love and light.
For it is here, I am released
from all the sadness this world brings.

Let me redeem into the glory
of your happiness and my own.

Lift me into the true infinite world of sanity
where happiness, peacefulness, safety, generosity,
unity, royalty and freedom dwell
for this would be divinely swell,
O my Lord.

Release me from the insanity
of the puny world of pains and sorrows.

We Suddenly See

In the light of your love,
we are one as we fit like a glove.

In the midst of joy,
you do not look upon us as a toy.

In the globe of your peace,
you ensure we succeed to awake
from the dream.

In the journey of your mercy,
you tenderly unveil the power
of your glorious clergy.

In the stillness of your grace,
you always show your lovely face
to remind us you are not fake.

In the lessons of your trust,
you ensure it does not turn to dust
for in the glory of your faith
you ease up all the dreadful pain.

In the spirit of your courage,
you ensure we are not discouraged
and in the glistening of your smile,
we are not defiled.

With a gesture of your hand,
you lead us to where we ought to stand,
for in the mangle of all the danger,
you show us we are no stranger.

In the sadness of earthly blues,
you give us the vision of Heavenly clues,
for this is how we remember
as we receive the message of our divine caretaker,
for it is only under the veil of love and light,
we shall see that fear and darkness
obscures all loveliness.
As we suddenly see the love and light of God,
we behold the innocence and beautification of Christ,
the peace and patience of the Holy Spirit,
the holiness and sinlessness of all the Sonship
and the loveliness of Heaven
all in One, as complete and certain.

As we receive the blessings
of love and light of He who is within,
we suddenly perceive what has always been.

Drunk in Peace

To offer a trinity of blessings all at once is a profound glory
under the love and light of God's delight in truth.

To elect to bless,
one can never go wrong.
To bless another's mess
with the word of God
is to confess His truth.

The double-edged sword of egotistic thinking
transforms sinful thought to holy thinking.
Indeed, peace befalls all parties involved.

When stillness transpires,
minds and hearts resonate holy fire.

Divine drunk in peace enters
where all one can do
is simmer in its well-oiled potent essence
taking in its blissful sovereignty.

In joy, body wavers yet the feet remain
planted ensuring not to stagger.

Being drunk in peace
is the holy instant when celestial forces enter.
Love and joy plunder willy-nilly
to ensure the full effect of nitty-gritty
upon the mind and heart.
The trinity dance of love, joy and peace
is certainly no fuddy-duddy.

One remembers, they are
simply and truly celestial buddies.

Drunk in peace is beyond anything
the world offers.
The enjoyment of it is so perfect,
no need to double check it.

The crux and flux of peace
is the deluxe of being drunk in peace.

This is what one can experience
when the choice is to bless the mess
of every situation and circumstance.

They enter with the dance of twirl and swirl
in celebration of one willing
to learn and remember the freedom of blessings.

Being at Home in Me

It has been so long
since I have felt at home in this world.

I have never felt at home
in this world.
I have always felt homesick
and could never figure out why
until my miracle happened.
2001 was the beginning
of my spiritual journey
to stop clowning around.

As a child, I can still remember
feeling so alien to this world.
My little world was so tiny,
yet I could never find any comfort
in the tiny space
I shared with my brothers and sisters.

For years, I lived inside a tunnel vision,
never being at home in me.
I was constantly uncomfortable
and restless in my own skin.
My only desire was to feel
comfortable and restful.
Instead, I felt homesick,
always trying to feel at home in me.

By the time, I reached adolescence,
the circle of discomfort was a vicious cycle.
This is where I grew completely blind
as I ran wild trying to escape from myself.

I wanted nothing more than to be
at peace with me
as I searched to find my place
in a world I felt I did not belong.

Then, one day, someone said to me,
"You cannot run from yourself
because you take yourself everywhere you go.
You must be willing to look inward
and there you find your home."

I understood the first part of what he said
and realized that he was right—
I do take myself everywhere I go!
Eventually, I did have to stop running from myself
but dismissed the second part of his phrase
because it was totally foreign to me.

He gave me a great piece of wisdom
but did not teach me to reach its freedom.
The tunnel vision I had spiraled deep down into
was narrow so I could not follow
the second part of his phrase
and never gave it a second thought.

Years later, as an adult
in a chapter of my spiritual walk,
I understood clearly what the second part
of this sentence meant—
my home is in me.

Yet, to this day,
I still endure feelings of homesickness,
much more intensely.
This has been
since my miracle with Christ.

Still trying to be at home in me
to finally rest in peace,
I traverse through earth and through
the rest of the chapters of my life
for whatever it is worth.
Then one night,
as I was getting ready for bed
I suddenly had a glimpse
of being at home in me.

It was such a comforting feeling
I had never felt on earth.
It stopped me still in my tracks…
I gazed around and said,
"Oh my goodness,
I feel at home in me!
What is going on, Lord?"

Joy followed the feeling
of being at home in me
and I was softly hurdled
into a quantum leap of
pure calmness and peacefulness.

O, how I never wanted it to cease
but I instinctively know it was a temporary glimpse
into the reminder of a gentle breeze of peace
I once danced with in Heaven.
We danced on water gracefully
without any kind of blunders.

The feeling of being at home in me
is the holy instant of God's hand upon me.
Just a touch of His fingertip
and I can feel His loving and tender vibes
reminding me of the peace yet to come.

Everyone here is a close friend of peace
and I bet even you had danced with peace
in the Kingdom of everyone's centerpiece.

This is the only empire
where rest and comfort never cease.

A Gentle Breeze of Peace

I remember the gentle breeze of peace
when I was in the realm of Heaven.

When I returned to earth
to wander through the past of time,
His gentle breeze softly dwindled
to honor me with the experience
of growing bitter.

Years later, through the event of being at home in me,
peace abolished the bitterness in me.
He entered and gave me a glimpse
of a gentle breeze of his essence to come.
This reminds me of a gentle breeze of peace
I danced with in Heaven.

After the encounter of being at home in me,
peace made a grandeur entrance
and returned to me three days later
when I received a package
that turned out to be
the publication of my first poetic book.

At the opening of the package,
a gentle breeze of peace swirled around me;
a breeze that is tenderly powerful
at the opening of the package
that my hair softly blew.
I danced around and thanked God
for all his wondrous blessings.

At his grand entrance,
joy joined in the excitement
and I absolutely love their divine climate.

For they filled up my cup
and cheered me right up
with overflowing joy and peace
that is a grandeur release of any excess
bitter-critters lingering within.
I am now in peace at home in me
because peace has fully entered
the loveliness in me.
Spirit, I forever keep.
Joy follows alongside of peace,
for in the world of time
they are exquisite realities and truths sublime.

A gentle breeze of peace
is the gift Christ brings
when I was feeling extremely homesick
as I attempted to feel at home in me.
In joy and peace, I wholly receive His gift
with appreciation and adoration.
His peace is a divine offering
as a congratulatory award to the publication
of my first poetic edition.

Little did I know,
He would gift me with further gifts of peace.

How Great Thou Art

It was the night of my 57th birthday
one stormy winter's night,
thunder thrashing, lightening flashing…

I was in the comfort of my home
all cozy and warm, candles flickering,
fireplace crackling as I watch an intense thriller
waiting for my Turkey dinner to get fully cooked.
Then a knock at my door breaks
the security of my solace.
I answer the door and he asks for water.
Of course, I was not going to deny him water.

As I turn away from the door to get him
a glass of water, he says,
"Ma'am, may I enter your home
to get warm?"

For a moment, I hesitate but then,
I remember this episode of my life script I agreed too
before I was even born.
So I permit him to come in to get nice and warm
even though I instinctively know it is a bad idea.
But, I also know this is the holy instant
I am to bless him even though I do not recall
how I am about to do that.

But when I turn my back,
he wraps his forearm around my neck.
Heck!
The blessing came rushing to my memory
in all clarity and certainty.

The memory permits me
not to resist.

I ask, instead,
"Before you do to me what you are about to do,
may I play a song?
Because if this is the last song
I will hear on this world,
let me listen to it as I perish at your hands."

He releases his forearm
from around my neck and says,
"Yes, you may."

So I play, *How Great Thou Art*
by Carrie Underwood with Vince Gill.

He falls to his knees
and pleas for God's forgiveness.
I tenderly wrap my arms around him
as I lay my cheek upon the crown of his head
and say,

"God has already forgiven you
for this episode of your life script
before you were even born
and I forgave you
before you even knocked at my door."

As he remains on bended knees,
he wraps his arms around me and says,
"Thank you."

I invite him in for dinner and he did eat.
He drinks the water as he sits
across the kitchen table
all warm and cozy.

He reaches for the doorknob,
but before he walks out the door,
he turns to ask,
"Did God really forgive me?"

I tenderly say,
"Yes, go and live out
the rest of your duration on earth
in righteousness and forgiveness
and you shall enter Heaven.
Let the Holy Spirit's perspective
of love, light, life and truth
bring you comfort and peace."

How Great Thou Art
touched him to the core
of his mind, heart and soul
releasing him in a holy instant
from the temptation of bad intentions.

I cannot stop the insensible
but with God, I can bless the inevitable.

Bad Seed Turned Good

Thoughts of the ego are bad seeds,
they flourish through the worship of every bad deed.

Its whole existence to its purpose
is to always have us thinking of ways to kill,
steal and destroy only to bind us
to its ugly and merciless ways.
There is another side to worship
that helps us embellish in merciful ways.
The miracle of true freedom
is the only way to abolish the demons inside.
The crazy idleness of all the violence going on,
constantly feeds Leviathan,
the most massive thing of its kind.
We show and tell of all its destructiveness
from all over the world enabling the power
of its wickedness to rise, this is its prize.
We worship judgment persecution,
conviction and imprisonment—
the ego's way of doing things.
We shackle the wrists and feet
locking humans up in iron cages
to curlicue its wicked ways.

Child of God, realize the bad seed within
is a ploy to get you to sin;
it is not your kin but the enemy within.
All it takes is a choice to either water or squash it.
Remember to refocus bad thoughts to good ones.
Hold the tongue of bad things to say
and refrain from acting out on thoughts of prey.
No longer bind yourself to ego's ways,
lift your hands and pray.

Forgive the evil slays and lift
its devastating behavior to the golden altar.
Let God do His miracles of healing
and correcting all falters of violence.
Step back in kindness, humbleness,
patience, peace and faith.
This is where we permit God to step in
to do His part of the greatest healing
and correcting through His miracles.
Here we are witness to the spark of the light within
when we let God do His part.
Blessings work both ways, we too are healed,
corrected and saved alongside our brothers.
We become witness to the blossoming
of the mind's wellness in all its holy wholesomeness.
This is where love, joy and peace rises.
All it takes is some willingness to listen
to the direction of the Holy Spirit's voice
where He always leads to the golden altar
where we lay the burdens of our brothers'
sick thinking and our own.
Good seed within is inevitably blessed
and awakens to true reality of who we truly are.
This is where we witness
the flourish of bad seed turned good.
God Himself unlocks the iron cage and throws away the key
so we can be free to spree in the restoration of redemption,
the healing and correction of mind.
To forgive the ego's behavior
and lift it up in prayer
upon God's golden feet at the Holy Spirit's lead,
let us witness God's swift miracles
of bad seed turned good.

*Here is where we behold the release of the chains and shackles
we put upon one to another.*

No Safety on the World

Through the agreement with all the Sonship
there is no safety on the world.

It is self-deception to believe
we can find a place to move to
on this world and be safe.
We agreed there would be thorns
planted at every corner of the world
where danger lurks everywhere we go.

This can be a rude awakening
or a gracious enlightenment depending on how
we elect to receive and perceive it.
To accept it for what it is
and learn to remember the deeper truth of it
brings peace.
The best way to do this
is to summon the Holy Spirit
because it is His goal to teach us
what is fabricated and what is factual
and this is what He is here for.

Deletion of illusion is to make room
for true answers to help us rise
to what truly matters.
The bosom of God's safety
is where the tremble of all aches
dissipates into nothingness.
When we escape into the darkness of the universe,
we still are not safe
because the universe houses dreadful explosions,
frozen and fiery deadly awesome dangers,
forces that constantly take their courses.

Yet, through love, light, life and truth,
there is life as we know it
deep into the universe that reaches
harmonic progression.
Their vibes are an undulation,
harmless and harmonious.

Even though there are deadly waves
of harmonic raves that would be
a challenge to dodge
all its chaotic bombardment of its frenzied music,
the good vibes outweigh the bad.
Remember it this way,
the only place where it is safe
is already within.
Safety is not outside of us
and it has always been this way
since time began.

All it takes is willingness
to dive into the psyche without being flighty.
It is nothing to fear because there are
no slight or sharp curves to run into.
There is nothing to despair
when we take the journey with the Holy Spirit.
As we reach the abyss of the mind,
we behold the openness of the golden altar of Heaven
where we instinctively know escape
to safety is possible
through bondable alignment with God.
The most beautiful brother
we will ever gaze our eyes upon is Christ
where He stands smiling ablaze
with open arms ready to embrace.

In the midst of His love and light
brings a pure, clean and fresh breath of air
knowing that we have found the only Kingdom
where there is safety and we know
we will be just fine.

There is no safety in this world
but you can escape it and you will
when you make the righteous choice
to learn and remember who you truly are
and where your home is.

Be willing to summon the Holy Spirit to assist you
in spiritual awakening of where true safety eternally lies.

Fearsome Movement

The sphere of the universe
has not always been so dark and barren,
a virgin atmosphere that is prevalent.

Its shimmer flows silently afloat
like a black sea of water
showering shadowy rainwater.
At the infancy of the veil of darkness,
it looks like a shimmery black sea
suspended in nothingness,
for there was nothing to liven it up
until under the laws of God's freedom,
He authorized the kick off to begin
worlds of miscreation, already planted
to commence its explosive
fearsome movement.

Upon the finish of universes' miscreations,
God enters and He lovingly and tenderly
outshines the space of the night,
sanctifies it with His love and light
before everything we made came to life.
His light of supreme power flourishes it
like wildflower,
for He is the tower of divine superpower
over everyone and everything He lovingly creates
under the open glistening golden light
of His divine soulmates.
His laws of freedom—to gloriously create
and ingloriously miscreate—
is generous to everything that blossoms.

For everything works out for the good in the end
and this is what His blessings did before time began.
He is righteous in all things
created under the holy shroud of love and light
and in all things made under the veil
of fear and dark.

Glorious creation is under the veil
of love and light that is
pure, clean, fresh, holy and sinless.
Inglorious making is under the veil
of fear and night which is
tainted, filthy, gory and sinful.
Under His laws of freedom,
He granted what we asked for.
Yet Heaven remains still,
while the universe commences
its fearsome movement.

While the dark circle of space expands,
we put into plan worlds of dreams
and everything else the darkness of the universe
houses in the vastness of its dreary fearsome circle
of its synthetic black matter of its biosphere.
The only thing realistic about the universe
is God's blessings He anointed upon it
while it was still barren even though to Him, it was foreign.
He sanctified the universe to be our friend
at the appointed time we choose
to let it work in our favor.
This is why, in the end,
everything always works out for the good
no matter how tragic things might seem.
In dream worlds, nothing is ever what it seems
and this is self-deceit.

In the advancement of its satin and buoyant biosphere,
the blackness is virgin no more
when synthetic worlds are explosively born
because we had torn our holiness away
from God and Heaven
to experience what we are not.
Explosions are symbolic
to the shattered souls of royal holiness
to be birthed into dream worlds
to witness and experience sinfulness,
the opposite of who we truly are.

God does not get even
because He permitted our souls befallen
because He knows we will return to Him
crawling, calling and screaming
at the moments we encounter events so insane,
we blame Him yet we call out His name.
The fearsome movement of outer space
is too great for us to bear alone.
This is where we want nothing more than
to come near to the safety of His bosom.

Fearsome movement engulfs humans,
but to forgive and atone
surpasses fear and darkness,
for our love and light tenderly combined
outshines the tremble of the heart.
Then, we behold the glorious eclipse
where we interlace with divine mercy and grace
and grip the spirit of miracles and principles
through our own vertical axis.

This is where we come to the full understanding of the proverb,
"Every cloud has a silver lining."

The Photo

(Dedicated to my lovely sisters who spoke telepathically without knowing it, Martha Rodriguez and Minnie Rodriguez)

She was looking for a photo
but could not find it anywhere,
when suddenly it appeared on her cell phone.

This happened without conscious awareness
of telepathic communication.
The sister who lived three hours away
heeded to the anxiety of the sister
failing to find the specific photo
she received on her cell phone.
She wondered how she'd known
she was seeking that photo.

The photo image was kind and sweet Granddaddy,
cradling his three month old granddaughter
looking upon her adorable face,
thrilled in the light of grace.
She looked for the photo
because she wanted to show to her niece
who is now grown and upbeat.
This is a neat sample of the telepathic example
because one sister did not know
the other sister was looking for that same photo.
We only trip upon the unfolding of the telepathic script
because we do not remember the day and hour it will enter.

Next time another brings you exactly
what you were thinking,
needing or seeking without you ever asking,
remember they are heeding the calling
of the script of telepathic thoughts from one to another.

They might not realize that moment has arrived
for what was already written to befall in its time.

'Tis the Season

While we sleep,
we dream of fear and darkness.

Looking at it through the eyes of the ego,
it wants nothing more than to ensure
we fear everything that appears frightful.
It says, "*'Tis the season to fear all things.*"
and "*'Tis the season to be jolly*" is no longer commonly used.
We elect phrases in the wrong context—
to bring fear upon another
but in this, we perceive through the eyes of the devil.
It is our enemy and is our greatest hater,
for it thrives and survives
through mistaken perception.

When we select phrases of goodness
to shine love, joy, and peace upon one another,
we stick to the white vine that intertwines
with a glistening golden lining of glue.
This is a quantum leap
enabling the ego thinking to be obsolete.
Holy thoughts emerge from invisible to visible
and this is the process of spiritual vision.
This is where we behold that it is love
that outshines all things frightening
until it fades into nothingness.
This phase heals and corrects perception
where it enables holy recognition
to the true meaning of 'Tis the season.

Always bring love, joy and peace upon one to another
from one side of the world to the other
extending and expanding it into the universe.

Amnesia

I was beaten and disheveled during the accident
that embezzled my long term memory.

Face first, I flew through the windshield
and though my face was not shattered
the windshield was hopelessly scattered—
a split from the left side of my hairline
to the right slope of my chin,
ankles, terribly mangled
while my long-term memory
slipped into amnesia.

Yet my short-term memory remained intact;
I was so young, I never felt any need
to regain the long-term memory
and this was a blessing because all it ever did
was shackle me to a ball and chain anyway.

Years later, I was struck by a big rig truck
which ignited the most important episodes
of my long term memory.
Through this incident, I regained
my spiritual vision and knowledge.
It took me on a trip through quantum leap
into my past, awakening me from being asleep.

Through this journey, I was shown episodes
from my long-term memory,
moments where I was loved
from the day I was born to the present.
This brought me great joy
in the midst of my recovery.

It was a blast of energy to my memory
these loving and precious moments
that amnesia had blocked for over twenty years.
To go through such brutal years
of feeling unworthy and unloved
is a very lonely place to be.
Through His miracle of quantum leap,
it was a swift way to release
the sensitivity of such defeat.

I felt safe in His light,
for it is the greatest love to find.
The love of His heart
was such a tender and cozy cushion,
that I could not wait to know my mission.
It was in this holy instant I understood
that this is most important.

The veil of amnesia was lifted
through the love and light
of God's miracle that showed me that
He had never left me through the brutality
of past, present and future experiences.

The miracle of His love
showed me the worthiness of my essence
and that love has always been my quintessence.

Doing the Time

We already did the crime,
this is why we are doing the time on Earth.

It is love we rebelled against
yet it is love we shall return too.
It will take willingness and courage
to reunite with our Father in Heaven.

Do not be frightened, little children,
for you will be enlightened
and wizened to your diamond star
suspended in Heaven.
At your willingness, you will gain courage to return
to thinking on a godzillion scale
where you will enter the realm of the miracle-minded.
This is where you will reach
the essence of divine kindness, humbleness,
patience and peacefulness which is pure bliss.
Through the guidance of the Holy Spirit,
you will rise from being
ruthlessly deaf, mindless and sightless.
Here, you reunite with righteous
in calmness and silence.
Your Heavenly glistening diamond star
shines balance upon righteous thinking,
for you are God's royal highness.
You will return to timelessness
for permitting God
to pluck the tyrant not of you.
Willingness to come out of defiance
is to be in alignment with the holy mind of God
as He honors your compliance,
for it is inherent.

Doing the time for our ancient crimes
is no punishment
because we are free to spree on Earth
until we return to the acknowledgment
of who we truly are.

Your majesty of redemption
cuddles you in embracement.
His divine love and light combines
His spiritual sight with your own
and lo and behold—
everything you want to know
is bestowed.

Blinders removed, behold divinely thoughtful,
no longer feeling lifeless.

The Great Escape

We could easily make things pleasant
and simple for each other.

But we choose to make things hard and complicated
because the ego in us thrives
on the complexity of destruction,
for it wants to see us suffer and tremble
through all the difficult challenges
of every prop that emerges
from the shadows of meadows
from all over the world and universes.

We are so blind to this
that we listen and follow its every wicked whim,
pushing aside the righteousness of
pleasantness—
the essence of simplicity.
We are the clay it molds
and we let it conform us to be ice cold,
for this is where we linger in its sufferings
as sad and pitiful fibbers.
We cry, shout and scream out for help
because we listen to the loud voice of evil
that is so puny, we barely notice it.

With its extremely loud voice,
we hear it loud and clear
and this is the voice we come to worship first
yet, we fail to realize
it leads to self-deception.
As long as we choose to listen to its puny thought system
that is so loudly annoying,
we throttle ourselves deeper and deeper
into the pit of self-destruction.

The deeper we spiral into its web of self-deception,
love and light is what we inevitably find at the center of it.
The loving essence full of mercy
is grace that pulls us out
of the tangled web of warped perception.
It is the ego's sinister prison
we strive and thrive to escape from.
This is where we inevitably scream out God's name,
for His shield and guidance to lead us out
from the pit of ego's darkness.
God's love, light, mercy and grace
is the one and only righteous way
to be free from negative thought network.

Through His tender sovereignty
is where we can find the great escape.

Madness of a Jester

Let me not frown or tremble in fear
under the madness of a jester who wears a permanent smile
but is so twisted inside in his insanity of sickness.

We all wear a mask to hide our foolish tasks,
for there is no difference between you and me.
We are alike in our foolish deeds.
Do not be a dead beat
in the madness of a jester.
Recognize the stupidity in what we agreed to,
as we perform what we were born into.
To behold the light inside
is to see the light in
whomever we are about to devour
while in the illusion
of wicked maneuvers of temptation.
Retreat from bad deeds
and let God water the beautiful seed
waiting to be nourished so it can flourish
in the loveliness of holy exquisiteness.
Be confident in being set free
from the cruelty, viciousness and horridness
of the performances we have the power
to renounce and bounce into holiness,
where we permit ourselves to thrive
as we strive to be born again
into the boldness of goodness.
In calmness, let the wicked storm pass,
for it is only a facade of the madness of a jester.
I promise you will fester
in the joyfulness, peacefulness,
sinlessness and guiltlessness of holiness.

Remember the agreement and forgive
to behold the righteousness
in all the Sonship and your own.
The madness of a jester
is a character in our life script
that we had agreed to act out or encounter.
To take the quantum leap
into holy wholesome remembrance
is a swift wonder to behold
and beyond everyone's wildest dreams.

God's light outshines all
so we may see what we are not,
altogether, in the madness of a jester.

The Opposite of Love and Light

We think the opposite of love is hate but the truth is—
the opposite of love is fear.

We fear because we are on a journey to find love.
We devour because we ache for love.
We corrupt because of the overwhelming desire
to reacquaint ourselves with love.
All the destruction we bring to others'
is because we fear them.
The urge to destroy them is because
we want to know them.
We degrade each other
because we crave the love of each other.
The ego is a veil upon the mind
to hide the love we have for God and each other.
Ego is made to steal, kill and destroy.
The total opposite of what love is.
Love returns what ego steals
He revives what the ego kills
and He sustains what the ego destroys.
Love is the Almighty God
who peacefully glides among us, unseen,
blessing every single one of us
with the glory of His generous gifting.
His gifts are the revival to the broken spirit ego,
that for a time, breaks down.

This is only an experience we agreed to encounter
where in the end, we remember,
God is the one who sustains the sovereignty inside
so we inevitably rise under the veil of love and light
where we find our way back to Him
escaping the ego's strongholds.

He walks among us unseen
because He is Spirit, yet so too are we,
but having a human experience.
We are blind temporarily to this
because we are too busy worshiping the body.
The evidence of it, is that we spend a lifetime
seeking Him outside of us
because we refuse to detect Him
when He is alongside of us.

The opposite of love is fear
and God did not create it,
we did, because we wanted to know
the opposite of what God is.

We made a loveless father
who will never give us what it stole from us.
It will never restore what it killed in us
and it will never sustain the love and light within us
because not only is it blind to it,
but it hates us.

The opposite of love and light
is fear and darkness.
God is love and light
and the ego is fear and darkness.

We spend a lifetime in fear
seeking God's love no matter the form it rises in
and we spend a lifetime seeking to see
because we are blind in the midst of darkness.

A Loveless Father

The idea of a loveless father
stemmed in Heaven through the perception
of a spoiled brat mentality.

We behaved in this way
because we asked for special treatment
that would cause separation.
God would not agree to this
because He knew
it would cause division among Heaven.

Changes of Heaven are not to be made
and this is how the creation
of a loveless father came to be.
We decided we wanted
to make our own father of complexity
because God himself is simplicity.

It is ironic that we do not fear
the loveless father
yet we fear God.
We are not brave enough
to love and save the holiness of the mind inside;
the nature of the ego is a coward
because God himself is courage.

There is no need to fear
for the Holy Spirit is here
to guide you out
of the weak grip of the ego.

Why is it weak?
Because God is strength.

It is better to learn
to dismiss the loveless father
who dictates our every thought
under the veil of negative forces.
It spins a web of wicked thinking
into harmful behavior
while we discount the love of God
we desire to acquire.
It is better to not replace
a loving Father with a loveless father
for it only brings horror and terror
upon ourselves and others.
To recognize the loveless father inside
is to see through spiritual eyes.

We must be willing to gaze
upon the love and light inside
and we will surely gain
the grace of God's embrace.
Here, there is no need
to fright, flight or fight the inevitable,
for God's true love is holy,
incredible and sensible
without the bondage of chains and shackles.

To relearn and remember
the loveless father we made is only a breath away
from our willingness to summon the Holy Spirit
to follow His lead towards redemption
which is in God's love and affection.

This is simplicity,
which is as easy as breathing.

Famous

We are stained with the wrath of pain,
for we wish to be noticed in a flurry of fame.

Yet it is time to tame the overwhelming desire
to be captured under the spotlight of false stature.
In the eyes of the Kingdom of Heaven,
we are all famous actors.
When the time arrives,
we will have our glory of fame
and all the Sonship will congratulate us
because this is what truly matters.

If worldly fame
does not come to pass in this lifetime,
rest assured,
it will arrive in another life.
However, in previous lives,
we may have already experienced
what it is like to be famous in illusional worlds.

Ultimately, fame in the eternal
is what matters most.

It is pleasing to gain control over this dream—
the overpowering yearn to be famous
because we will get our glorious fame
when we return to Heaven.
This is a much more festive celebration
than the glory of fame that the world offers.

We let our irresistible emotions
of becoming famous consume us,
because we do not remember
we are already famous from the moment
we are born from Heaven to earth.
When we return to the Kingdom from which we belong,
we are congratulated and crowned
for our great performances
and experiences we endured on earth.
We are already a glory of fame and life in Heaven is no game
for the day will arrive for all to see we are famous in the eyes
of Him.
For God Himself crowns us with the golden crown of eternity
when we make it out of the maze of the ego's sinister prison.
This is the greatest escape we will ever accomplish
on every dream world we are born in.

From the time we are born,
we are already famous, worshipped and praised
because we made it safely out of a world
where its foundation was built on
fear, darkness, guilt, conviction, judgment,
punishment, imprisonment, confusion, chaos and self-deceit.
To return to Heaven through Christ's atonement
in forgiveness, love, joy and peace is redemption
and what makes us a glorious famous superstar
where our celestial diamond star is suspended
in the skies of Heaven that glistens for all eternity;
a token of God's golden congratulations
to the status of our celebrity state.

This is greater than the star plastered on the ground
where everyone continuously steps, stomps and walks upon it
not really genuinely admiring it.

Reoccurring Dream

In a reoccurring dream, there is a house
that has three doorways, but no doors.

The three doorways are entrances to the house
and anyone has access to me at any given moment.
I seek to attempt to hire a door installer
but no door installer was willing to help me.
I grew more and more desperate
to get three doors installed
so I would feel safe.

Even though people around me
were very friendly,
I desperately wanted doors.
I was timid and very suspicious
because I felt unsafe.
I called around to family and friends
to try and go stay with them
but no one ever answered their phone.
I felt trapped among friendly neighbors
who welcomed themselves into my home
their attitude was as if this was natural
no knocking at the threshold's open doorways.

Although they were friendly,
in my mind, I am suspicious of their friendliness
and all I could think is that their pleasantness
is a more sinister plot to get me;
I instinctively know
they can read my thoughts.
This compelled them
to compassionately look into my frightened eyes,
smile and turn around and walkaway.

This is what every visitor did
after reading my suspicious thoughts.
Something within me wants to see deeper
into the meaning of these people
that know what I am thinking.
As I wake from this revolving dream,
I do not attempt to figure out the meaning of it.
But what kept reoccurring in dreams,
was the memory of the three open entrances
to the doorways of my house.

"It was just a dream," I thought.
But when I awake from this dream,
I know I awoke to another dream
where I feel a more intense fear
and discomfort of feeling unsafe.
I knew no matter which way I turn to wake
as long as I am on earth and in time,
I am going to keep dreaming
until I elect to spiritually awake
or my spirit transitions from Earth to Heaven
where I instinctively know
I will find love's eternal safety.

The dream world I live in,
family and friends forsake.
People tell you they love you
but eventually they turn on you
and abandon you.

But I remember these are
experiences we asked for
and we receive what we ask.
Therefore, there is no one to blame.
It is willingness to forgive what is important
because we all agreed to it.

With God's Holy Spirit, I came to the conclusion
that the reoccurring dream of the house I was living in
without three doors to the entrances of my home
is symbolic to the way it is in Heaven.
The kingdoms in Heaven we created
are full of many rooms with no doors
to close, lock or knock on.

Doors and locks are not needed in Heaven
because we are forever safe,
for no one ever forsakes.
We are welcomed,
walking into kingdoms freely
because we are all love and light.
Welcoming one another
into our kingdoms is natural
and this is how it is in Heaven.

On earth, we build houses with doors and locks
because in dreams we do not welcome one to another.
We prefer to install doors and utilize locks
to put a block to anyone entering
because in dreams
we are not safe from each other.

Subconsciously, we remember God's safety
but we constantly deny it
by not welcoming strangers or each other
even though we are all brothers.
We elect to not exercise faith in God
even though with Him, we are safe.

In the reality of dreams,
we install doors and locks
so no one enters without permission;
the attempt to feel safe.

Yet eventually, we learn there is no safety
in every corner of the globe in dreams
even when we lock windows and doors,
we still are not safe.

There is nothing to fear in Heaven
because there it is natural to forever welcome
one another into our kingdoms.

This is how it is
under the cover of God's love and light
where everything is open including our thoughts
and this is why we are openly telepathic
in our thinking of the majesty of Heaven.

This reoccurring dream I no longer have
is symbolic to the way it is in Heaven.

Bottomless Thirst

In the physical, unnatural world,
we thirst for everything.

We want endless life, youth, beauty,
money and materialistic things
that wither, rust and turn to dust.
We lust for all the things
we already have and always had
that we temporarily forget about.
Let divinity tenderly twirl
a gust of wind to help you bust out
of the realm of bottomless thirst.
Trust the Trinity to sprinkle upon
the crown of your head a glistening
of golden stardust that never withers,
rusts and turns to dust.

No longer be active in antitrust.
Let the Holy Spirit divinely adjust your thinking
to the correction of the remembrance
of the deed of trust you signed
before you were even born.
To trust in the Trinity
enables them to pluck you out
of the pit of bottomless thirst.
The very curse you cast yourself into
only to experience the events of death
that in the end,
lifts your coffin into a hearse.
Yet at that moment of departure from the body,
the spirit is tenderly hoisted skyward
where you witness the outburst of sadness
of those who will miss you dearly.

They do not recall
they will see you again in a world
where suffering and loss
does not exist.
But you in spirit see clearly
there is nothing to be sad about,
for you are no longer
in the realm of bottomless thirst;
you are back home
where that thirst is quenched
through the cinch of breath.
The bottomless thirst is an illusion
but beyond the universe is the reality of Heaven
where you are never deprived of anything.

All your treasures are endless,
never to wither, rust and turn to dust.

Confusion

Confusion is not of God.
Yet, we live in a world where confusion rules.

Willingness to learn the truth
is what is going to unravel
all confusion of the illusional impressions
we see through optical vision.
Let the mind unwind the confusion of time
and allow it to disconnect
to let truth interconnect
where we behold the beauty
of timelessness.

It can be achieved in the world of dreams
which brings the Kingdom of Heaven
into spiritual vision.
We interlace with the inviting of grace.
God's decency lets it be
where everyone remembers joy and peace.

Spirits lifted as we yearn to learn
how to not sink down.
We are in the era to finally care
for the most delightfulness of holiness
in all its fullness outshining the darkness
of sinfulness.

Swiftly, the quantum leap brings with it—
self-awareness into spiritual vision
to finally dwell in wakefulness
where the confusion unravels
and everything comes together.

To embrace spiritual knowledge
is to behold everyone and everything
that is flawless—
the essence of holiness and sinlessness.

Confusion is not of God
and this means neither should it be part of you.
He created you in His likeness.

Willingness to learn perfection
is in His holiness
which sanctifies happiness and peacefulness
on a grandeur scale
where you will tell the glorious tales
of God's miracles and your own.

One and the Same

Competing with one another in events of competition
battling in the race to win, rattling the ego's sin.

Groups in a contest
struggle to befriend each other
because they believe they are there
to win and not make friends.
The ego stews jealousy brews,
anger boils over in the scuffle
to compete in the hustle.
The name announced for the best test,
and the opponent smirks a smile at the winner.
The fallen one gives a subtle jerk
trying not to show it, as to not blow it.

Yet, we do not remember
that there is no such thing as defeat
when we compete.
We are all winners
even if you think you are a loser
because we are one and the same
in such loveless games.
God tells us not to covet another's trophy,
look at it as your own glory.

Remember we are one and the same
and one day, we will see
we are all winners.
Truly, no one is a loser.

In the end, God crowns each and every one of us
at His throne with the crown of eternity
because it is everyone's destiny.

Every Child of God Is...

The King of Creation is like a breath of fresh air,
feelings of elation when He reaches down with His fingertip
as you lay or sit just to give you a fraction of His love
as a reminder of who you truly are.

His touch is as velvety as Heaven's melody
most enticing so inviting and exciting.
His Holy Spirit always guides you
to who you truly are
as He leads you out of the nightmare
we all created to experience;
all it takes is one ask.

It is only through His lead
unification sprouts like weeds.
It takes no hard work at all on your part,
because love and light is already planted within
godzillions ago.
All it takes is willingness,
diligence, vigilance and consistency.
Every child of God is worthy
of His divine serenity,
for we are created by God
and He is love and light as are we.

It is best to never cease
to seek the way out
of what we enslave ourselves to,
for we are children of God
remaining free forever.

To claim your inheritance of true freedom
and wake from Adams's dream and your own
is the glory of *te deum.*

Every child of God is priceless
because we are created in His likeness.
It is best to no longer be mindless.
All it takes is willingness
to let wisdom flourish.
The God we know never needs a spaceship
to get from one point to another
We too don't need a spacecraft
to get from one place to another
if we would only let the light inside shine through.

The light in you lifts you up
for it is the gravity of travel
where there is no grain of gravel.
The golden road to Heaven is velvety smooth.
Bring your brothers with you
for every child of God is spirit
and together, our combined light is so powerful,
we can be everywhere all at once just as God is.
Every child of God is the Sonship
created to unite in love, light, life and truth
where friendship, joyfulness and peacefulness elbows.
The atonement in that moment
is a universal contentment
because we reconcile with Christ
who is our brother in Heaven.

*Every child of God is priceless because every soul is His creation
and we are delighted to remember this through our willingness
to behold it through the eyes of the Holy Spirit.*

To Put It Bluntly

To put it bluntly, we are all deranged.

The lifestyle of others we look upon
is because it's too painful
to look at our own.

Playing the game of defilement is a form of control
through the dictation of ambivalence;
the equivalent of catering
to our own insecurities.
This is a form of fear
of losing our own purities
yet, we can never lose
the purity of divinity
and in holiness, we truly are.

Putting labels on one another
is because name calling
was already placed on the table
before we were even born.

We point fingers and blame one another
because we want to stay in denial
because we don't want to take a look
at our own guilt and shame;
playing sick games shows
how we are mindfully the same.
To protest is the hope of a show
to gain respect, acceptance and change.
To look past flesh and bones
is to behold the value of what is most important.
This is where we remember
we are not so foreign.

The spirit leaps in joy
recognizing what is most endearing.
This is where we rise beyond the clouds
watching all the confusion on the ground.
To return to a healthy perception
is to be spiritually reborn
by forgiving everyone and everything
that left us feeling torn and scorned.

To learn the true meaning
of loving and caring for one another
with the upmost respect, acceptance, integrity and dignity
is to be merciful, to put it bluntly.

This is the divine change we seek
and when we return to love and peace,
we clearly see, we are the same.
No longer a merciless game,
but a merciful reclaim to the true you.

To put it bluntly, this is where nothing else matters
because we remember all the fuss of illusion
is all going to go up in smoke anyway.
Every chance is given to receive restoration
of a sad and crushed spirit.
It is okay to receive
the glistening golden yoke
of who we truly are.
Having the choice to go out
of this world in a blaze of glory
is an honor.

To put it bluntly, through divinity,
we are all of sound mind
once we finally find what truly matters.

This is where we are honored
to learn respect and accept one another
as we look past every mindless blunder.
Humanity is designed to be imperfect.
This is where we remember,
it will all be dismembered.
To put it bluntly,
it is up to every single individual
to learn and remember
what is real and what is imagined.
To put it bluntly, it is through spirituality,
we learn to treat one another
with love, respectability, acceptability, integrity and dignity,
which is pure decency.
This enables forgiveness, kindness, humbleness,
patience, peace and faith
to enter under the veil
of love, light, life and truth—
God's ultimate miracles.
To put it bluntly, this is the primary change
we all seek but we cannot achieve it
through physical perception.
We must be willing to adopt spiritual vision.

To put it bluntly, we are not deranged,
we are divinely aligned.

No Need for Privacy

Heaven is pure, fresh and clean
nothing ever needs to be
dusted, buffed, washed, painted,
polished, vacuumed or watered.

Everything is alive, well and sparkly clean
because God's light is so bright
that not even a mischievous speck
of microscopic particle can enter Heaven.

There is never any need
to hunger or thirst because
breathing in the lovely aroma of food
and drinks quenches hunger and thirst.
There is never any need
to digest, pee and poop,
not even burp or fart.
There is never any need
to shower, wash or brush your hair
because it is forever sparkly clean
and fresh all the time
just as it is everywhere
in Heaven's atmosphere.
Purity is so divinely satisfying
in Heaven that sex is non-existent
and the crave for privacy is not needed.
We are free to be
in Heaven.
The mind is completely open
because everything in Heaven is shared
even our thoughts
because this is the freedom
with the openness of the mind.

Complete holiness,
wholeness and wholesomeness
is the way of immortality
in the Heavenly Kingdom's true reality.

In Heaven, everything is wide open
from microscopic life forms
to the mind, heart and soul.
As an immortal, we are forever
under the safety of God's cover
where there is no need for privacy
the essence of true freedom.

Every life form shows their celestial true colors
like the open golden glistening rainbow
in the skies of Heaven.

My Love and Care Is with You

Take solace in the truth,
for all experiences of pains and sorrows are illusions.

Therefore, they are not truly happening.
It feels like it is because you feel
the consequences of it.
In spite of this,
everything you experience
through the perspective of the ego
is all an act.

Every single one of you
are bright shining diamond super stars.
You are the star of your own movie.
Learn to remember,
you are merely acting.
Remember, even actors on earth
experience fear and get hurt
while they are filming their movies.
However, they might be at peace
and accept it for what it is
because they remember
they are acting.

Experiencing the illusions
on this world is no different.
When you remember your Father in Heaven,
you will behold the super star
you truly are.

"Child of light, I remind each and every one of you,
the insanity of your mind will be fully restored.
Remember that your mind and spirt
are safely in my hands.
In the end, all the glory of what you will receive
is abundantly beyond what you can behold
and know at this time.

Always let yourself remember
that I understand your tears and heartaches
to all you think you have lost.
All the hurt and pain
through every sad devastation
you think you are witnessing
is happening all around you.

I assure you, my child,
all the royalties of your lovely
and beautiful creations you created
before you were even born
is in Heaven, safely guarded,
awaiting your return home.

Do not despair
for I am handling every soul with love and care
as well as your eternal treasures.

Be patient little while more
in kindness, humbleness, patience and peace.
For the blessings of your heart's desire
to remember the love, light, life and truth
of the safety of the golden circle you seek—
in a holy instant, I assure you
I will pour upon your memory.

My love and care is with you.
Peace be blessed upon you
through your duration of time
until your return home."

Remain calm through every endeavor
and invite Him in and He shall
wipe away your tears
as He blesses the spirit of stillness
upon your dreams.

Through every experience,
remember the illusion
when you feel its graphic affects
and its sound effects
particularly the pain and sorrow
of your own events.

Do not boggle your mind with all the whys
because you are merely acting.

My Thoughts

The character of the ego
is to ensure we uphold fear.

It exercises the evil depths
of its darkness
keeping us in bondage
with its destruction and death
to make certain
we never behold and know
the golden circle of light
i n s i d e
that tenderly outshines it
enabling us to see
the beauty of the immortality within.

In the end, God's golden light
overflows in everyone and everything
where we are witnesses
to the truth of immortality.

The Kingdom of Heaven has been us
since the beginning of creation and time
and it will triumph.

A Soft Whisper

I am nine years old
Papa rules the household with an iron fist
would yell at me if I resist.

As he sits on the couch
mumbling and grumbling nonsense,
I tiptoe behind him.
I take the tip of my index finger
to meet the tip of my thumb
and give him a flick
upon his pointy ear.
It shuts him up
and he looks up stunned
as he fixes his puny eyes
upon my funny gesture.
I giggle but I wonder if
he would backhand or ground me.
For weeks I could not
go out and play;
my jolly child's play,
he saw as
a doggedly faulty joke.

I sit on the old raggedy couch
in front of the big bay window
watching all the other kids' play
as I roll a ball of clay
between the palms of my hands.
Papa's tone of voice sounded annoyed
when he said,

"I am going out and you better not
go outside and play about!
If you do, a paddle,
you'd get on your behind!"
I give no thought
to such a ridiculous threat
and run outside the moment he left.
I freely play with my neighborhood friends
when my big brother said,
"I will keep an eye out for Papa."

I shrug my shoulders
for I do not care.
I smile happily as I blissfully play
with my childhood neighbors.

My big brother suddenly shouts,
"Here comes Papa,
you better get in the house!"

I hunch my shoulders and giggle
as I run to climb the leaf-filled tree
in front of our house.
I dare not run in the house,
for fear of being confined
and trapped like a mouse.

Papa drives up onto the driveway, gets out
of the car and there I am up in the leaf-filled
tree as I watch him walk into the house.

Quickly, he storms out of the house
and shouts out my name.
I watch, I listen and I giggle
my hand over my mouth
so as to not give him
a clue as to where I am about.

Papa angrily shouts out to my big brother,
"Where is your sister?"

My brothers lips pucker,
he shrugs his shoulders
as if he did not know
that I am up in
the leaf-filled tree.

Papa's ridiculous anger
uproars in his head
as the ego uses his mouthpiece
to curse and threaten as he seeks me out
never looking up the tree.

Suddenly, I hear a soft whisper
it grabs my attention
and I stretch my neck
to look further up the tree
to try and see who spoke to me.
I stay planted on the tree trunk
for I dare not flee
the safety of the tree.

As I search for the whisper,
Papa's furious voice becomes fainter.
As I look further up the tree,
I do not see a thing.
I look upon the crown of Papa's head
when a soft whisper at my ear says,

"Have faith in the lovely things
you do not yet see,
for I am your Father in Heaven,
the Spirit in you and you in me.
I am always with you
and I love you for all eternity."

Such tender love and cozy warmth engulfs me
as I listen to the soft whisper
from within this tree.

I relax and lay my head
upon a branch, simmering…
I have never felt this majestic peace
in my chaotic little world before.

Papa's enraged speech collapses into violence
but I rest in complete calmness and silence
under this soft whisper's guidance
up in the leaf-filled
tree all snug and free.

I tune out Papa's fuming voice
and remain in the leaf-filled tree
under the veil of sweet love and peace.

My faith is bound to this soft whisper
from our Father in Heaven
and is greater than Papa's hostile uproar.

His Presence

When I drift away in distraught
He brings me back to glorious thought.

Back in the day,
getting my attention was a long shot
because as an atheist,
I thought I was a big shot.

An attitude of fraught
swiftly transforms to being
totally lost.
I remember being self-centered
and how quickly I was tempered.
Being lost
was like a pressure cooker that burst,
but it was no curse.

I fell into a deep sleep
where He awakened me—
I collapsed to my knees
in surrender…
not by force,
but by His love, endorsed.
His presence so powerfully pleasant
even though I am a peasant.
I thank Him for the spirit of awakening
and for being with me through
every phase of my destiny.

His presence is the gift
that brings me back when I drift.

Follow the Glistening Golden Road

Follow the glistening golden road
for it decodes everything
you ever want to behold and know.

As you walk alongside the Holy Spirit
on the glistening golden road
He will tenderly unravel
every episode of your life script,
brilliantly unraveling
the truth from the false.

It is a divine trip to watch
before your very eyes
as each clip unravels
to help you get a true grip
on the things you agreed to
write, make and bring
to this synthetic life—
it washes away all the pain.
Gently, you are hurdled
above the vastness of galactic
where it all clicks in your memory—
divinely, cleverly, swiftly
but tenderly.

Here, you can behold everything
you have ever known,
for the blindfold will be fully removed
if you were bold enough to pass the threshold
of the glistening golden road to Heaven.

In that holy instant, you will drop
all the world's synthetic baggage
and in that moment,
courage will enter
to help you come out
of the bondage
of the devil's sinister prison.

Everything that is a blur
will now become clear as crystal,
for you will absolutely concur
with everything you yearn to remember.
It is not a bleak bummer,
it is as sweet as honey amber;
opening memory of every somber
into the love and light of the glory
of being happily and peacefully sober.

Follow the glistening golden road
that offers truthful answers.

Part 2
Golden Worlds

The only time we can know that the point of no return does not exist is when we behold the truth and false of everything seen and unseen.

Courage

Worlds of illusion bring about
devastations of fearful confusions.

Deep in our mind and heart,
we know illusions
are senseless and meaningless
because it offers sufferings
mixed in with pleasures
and we all know—
pleasures outrank sufferings!

Even those who bring pain
and suffering upon others' do not like to suffer.
When the tables are turned,
they will plea for you to stop
and let them live just as you did.
Yet, it does not matter
who brings about pain and suffering
because we all do it, regardless
of the form it rises in.

Have courage, be bold and fear not,
for this enables you to behold
the essence of faith and hope.
Let God remove the blindfold,
release the stronghold and be blessed godzillion fold.
Under the divine power of courage
enters the spirit of kindness and humbleness
outshining the dark within and lets everyone live.

The essence of courage is kindness,
humbleness and patience
which is the center of love, joy and peace.

Gifts planted inside godzillions
ago at the core of mind, heart and soul.

Dreary Fearsome Circle

There is always a long list of questions
as to where this false direction leads.

Shadows of the past
are simply reflections of deception
pointing to a false direction,
ensuring we look away
from the Kingdom of Heaven.

Through its warped perception,
we believe in its deceptive dreary fearsome circle
that houses a string of treachery tales.

Through every road taken,
we run into frightful figures
and have worldly expectations
in every deceitful and friendly expression.

We are so blind, we do not behold
the love and light in every glorious smile
or what seems like a devious one.

To learn to release
from the frown of seriousness as we traverse
through the shadows of the past
is true freedom.

In every experience we come upon,
we have forgotten that love and light
is at the center of every figure we encounter
no matter how strange and bizarre
it arises in.

Every shooting star is symbolic
to every soul zooming through
the vast darkness of the universe,
eager to make a grand entrance
to their fairytale menace.

We cannot even wrap our minds
beyond the number trillion
because the menace feels endless
from the moment, the troublemaker
started it godzillions ago.
We do not remember this
because every life scattered
has a genetic code
that goes so far beyond the moon.

Be willing to emerge
from the dreary fearsome circle
to no longer experience shadows of the past.

Grow a backbone and learn to remember
your Heavenly château from godzillions ago.

We made the strange and bizarre, even the blazing stars.
What we think we see outside of us
is a reflection of what is part of us.

Gifts

Christ arrives at the appointed time…

We asked Him to enter our realm
to assist us in recalling Him and Heaven
as part of God's miracle
to begin to heal and correct cynical minds.

When He enters,
He never arrives empty handed.

Far too often, we ignore His presence
because we are too wrapped up
in the ego's loud voice
and puny visions.

This clogs our senses and blinds us
to the gifts He lays at our feet.

Because we are in agreement,
He crosses over with gifts
to help us recall who we are
and where we come from.

He awaits in patience and peace
for you to receive.

His gifts remain at our feet
until we are ready to behold them,
for God gives but never takes away the gifts
He has already given
at the event of creation.

God is royalty and this makes us imperial
because He is our creator.

His gifts are already ours
and always have been since godzillions ago,
but we have forgotten this long ago.

When we give gifts to another,
we must do as God does.

It is honorable
to never take back what we give
no matter how angry
we get with one another.

Gifts are blessings, particularly,
when we give and receive from the heart.

As the receiver,
it is majestic to be thankful
and grateful to gifts
we accept from others.

When time enters to recognize
gifts from Christ, we see this clearly.

We behold and know
in all clarity and certainty
that He never retrieves them
no matter our behavior,
for in Him, there is no madness,
only gladness.

It is divine to behold gifts
that come from the heart of God and your own.

We give gifts to one another

to express our thankfulness and gratefulness
for something wonderful someone else did
to help us through any situation.

However, too often, the receiver
does not respond appreciatively.

When Christ enters with His gifts,
can we recall all the times
we did not respond gratefully?
This is only because we are blind
to His presence.

He is invisible
but He understands this.

We are physically ungrateful to the giver
because we are blind to the glorious purpose of giving
even though we can physically see the gift
but when the time enters to behold
your gifts from Christ and its true purpose,
it becomes easy for us to accept
those who do not respond
to our gifts favorably.

We recognize they are blind
to the purpose of our kind gestures
and are able to move forward.

When the giver gives as God does from the heart
and the receiver does not respond with gratitude,
they perceive it through the eyes of the ego
and not through the perception of the Holy Spirit.

Every gift that comes from the heart of God
and your own is priceless
and every gift that comes from the ego's dictation
of manipulation is worthless.
Holy gifts unveil the remembrance
of whom God and Heaven is,
who we are
and where our home is.

Christ's gifts are the most meaningful
because they are gifts of royalty
and grace to humanity.

Over the Threshold

When all feet step over the threshold,
there is an instant of restoration.

Merciless thinkers have no qualms;
they trespass, hiding behind computer screens
behaving in sinister ways.

They search and swerve
through its electronic brain
hunting whom they can devour.
Like evilness lurking in the shadows
waiting to pounce, not giving an ounce
of care for one's privacy or safety to bear.

Through the experience of every dreamer
whether victim or victor,
Christ always holds the doors wide open
for everyone to enter.
The day comes when every footstep
emerges from darkness
to cross the threshold into holiness.

Instantly, every eye sees,
every tongue confesses
and every gesture shows the boldness
of the true reality of Christ and Heaven.

All the ruthless coldness is tossed aside,
as the merciful spirit enters to be a witness
to our merciless pride vaporizing into oblivion.

This is such a pleasurable moment
displaying an ear to ear smile in the recognition
of who you truly are
and the world which you come from.

To behold such a majestic Kingdom,
divorces the marriage of the ego's negative forces.
because there is an instance of restoration
from insanity to sanity,
mortality to immorality,
sinfulness to holiness
and from earth to Heaven,
the Kingdom that always beckons
minds to awaken.

When all feet step over the threshold,
there is an instant of restoration.

Ability in Every Mind

Everything that unfolds in worlds of illusion
has already been prewritten before time ignited.

Scientists who study the universe
do so through their own prewritten life script.
They must be among us, scientists
who study the universe through spiritual vision.
If they are, I hope they will emerge
from the woodwork in my lifetime.

Everyone prewrote their own life script.
It would be nice if we all knew this
because the moment that we do,
we can get a grip of our minds
and learn to encrypt on an ethereal level.
By our own making, we agreed to be
born into worlds of crazy.

When we first hear this, our eyes get lazy
and the mind gets hazy.
I hand you a lily, invite you to get brainy.
No need to get hasty as it is very easy.
It is the ability in every mind
to no longer be blind.
Everything we've always known
is all bundled up inside,
seeping through dreams
every time we go nighty-night.

We are co-authors,
but also cocreators and co-makers.
This is the one reason we cohabit.

It would be nice to spiritually synchronize
so each of us can reach
a peaceful and harmonious demise.
I say this to all the scientists who study the universe
and have made it their life goal
to know it through illusional physics,.
You have an enormous advantage
to instantly know how the universe works.
You can do this through spiritual vision.
To look at everything you have ever studied
through the illusional context
all comes together in a holy instant
when you view it through God's eyes.

This is true for each and every one of you.
Just ask the Holy Spirit
to take you on a divine ride
through quantum leap
to be shown all that you wish to know
as it all comes together in a heartbeat.

Through the ability of every mind,
there comes an exciting time that fills you
with an overwhelming eagerness
to share this divine knowledge
with all the world.
After all, it does supersede the greed
to keep it all to yourself.
Be willing to be open to this
as it certainly flourishes to the true genius inside.

The ability in every mind is where you find
the glistening golden circle inside.

Mr. Rugged

Mr. Rugged sat on a bucket,
his strings were pulled as if he were a puppet.

His desires of destructible action,
I did not acquire
as it requires a self-destructive bonfire.
I pick up a pail of water
and splash it onto his flaming blame.
He has no shame in giving false blame.
There is only false in what looks to be cruel
and he gets his fuel from his desire to duel.

O Mr. Rugged, who sits on a bucket,
no longer be a fool from your desire to duel.
Calm down and be cool,
learn the tools in the testament of truth.
Step out of the false game
and into the glory of true fame.

Here, you can bear the heaviness of strife,
lay down the knife and live your life
in the glory of love and light.
No need to duel,
for you are wasting your fuel.
Step out of the dark and into the light
and be a delight.
Go and be the true you.

You will see
this is where you are to be,
for the silly rubbish will
only cause you to become sluggish.

Reserve your fuel to the goodness in you,
for you will be motivated to the end of time
as long as you choose to lay down the crime.

Come to the divine
and lay your sword upon His shrine.
This is where you behold the worthiness
of your holiness already in you.
Rest in righteousness
to reach the realm of happiness.
This is the atonement of Christ's holiness,
humbleness and peacefulness that has always been inside.

O Mr. Rugged, hallelujah! Tenderly, He zaps the desires
of the fuel because the duel truly is not of him.

The Memory of You

Ever since I met you,
I have not once stopped thinking of you.

From the day I met you I knew
I was in your Holy presence
and the memory of you I want to keep
without ever letting go.

The day I looked upon your handsome and lovely face
was the day the memory of you
came dashing into my mind
like a flowing river,
glistening golden, tender and sweet.

I want to keep the memory of you forever
because I remember you were
never the deceiver and disconnector.
You are the giver and savior
and I am the receiver who gives to you in return
my loyal love, sweetly and permanently.

I commit my loyalty to you endlessly
because long ago,
you dedicated your devotion to me eternally.
I want the memory of you forever.

You are not the loyal breaker
but I was the heartbreaker
and turned my back on the tears you shed
and fled as if I did not care
that I had broken your tender heart.

Here, I went hurdling down a spiral,
tumbling as I heard your voice calling me back.

But I did not want to return to you
because I thought I was correct at best.
As I spun deeper down the spiral
from the divine Kingdom of which I fell,
the light I knew faded more and more
as everything around me
became a dark blackness of nothingness.

My eyes gaze upon a ground
of which I softly land,
as I rise from bended knees,
my eyes circle upon an unrecognized world
where I find myself surrounded
in a misty fog of darkness
with black trees and gray leaves,
such a gloomy place to be.

When my eyes gaze upon the awareness of me,
I could clearly see the dimness of the light
I knew in me.
I swiftly understood that
to break your heart and leave you,
the light in me separated from you.

This, you did explain would happen
but I chose to fall like a burning flame anyway
only to land into a world of darkness
where I would experience
phases of fear and sadness.

I screamed out your name
because I instinctively know that
without you there is no light.
Without the connection to you,
I find I do not shine so bright.

I am relieved to see,
you did not and would not
cut the glistening golden umbilical cord
enabling me to find my way back to you
where I clearly behold and know in all certainty
that I want the memory of you forevermore.

I am more grateful than I ever have been
you did not bring me back to you,
forcing me to stay with you.
By letting me fall, it gave me a clearer insight
of your devoted call from the core of your tender heart.
I forgive you for letting me spiral out of control
and I forgive myself for breaking your tender heart
and I forgive the Sonship because I am not alone
in this decision to break your heart and leave you.

I agreed to disconnect from your Holy presence
and I thank you for graciously keeping your promise to me
that the power of your love and light
shines upon and through my mind to be shared
all over the world and into the universe.
I humbly connect with you relentlessly,
O Father in Heaven
because I cannot do this without you.
Therefore, I want the memory of you forever.

In gratitude, I humbly identify in certitude,
I am lost without you.

Earth

There was no such thing as a universe.

We made the darkened world
that houses earth and all the other illusional worlds
we know of and have not yet discovered.

The problem on earth lies deeper than we remember.
The belief that every tragic episode
we ourselves prewrote and premade
is where anger and depression stems from.

Through memory loss,
we point fingers and blame one another
only to toss aside the lessons we need to learn
and remember through every endeavor.

We do not recall the agreement we all were sworn into
by our own willingness to be born as experiencers.
In humbleness, we honored forgiveness
from one to another while still in Heaven.
We bowed our heads and peacefully forgave
knowing the illusion would inevitably cave.

Yet, we prayed
we'd honor forgiveness from one to another,
for the illusions we will be born into
would bring much strife to one another
and not remembering it is an act
that will not last forever.

The brutality of the reality of illusion
are fabricated acts to cause devastation and confusion.

Through distorted laws,
we attempt to keep it all intact,
but it all goes whack when we forget to forgive
all that we agreed to begotten.

Our tummies twirl and knot
to all the destruction pre-plotted.
We spend a lifetime seeking to connect the dots
trying to make sense of the misbegotten.
It is a miscreation designed to spiral into damnation.

Even damnation is illusion
but willingness is key to regain spiritual cognition
into the celestial world of vertical thinking
to no longer cling into the hell of horizontal thinking
where we go down sinking.
Stop squinting and pen your eyes to begin winning.
Only through God's eyes
can we behold the spirit of forgiveness.
Here, He opens the portal of quantum leap
and trust me, you will not weep.
This swiftly awakens memory loss from sleep,
a memory gain to forever keep.
Because you see, forgiveness is key
to bring us out of misery.
The choice is yours and it always has been.

The chains and shackles of the ego's sinister prison
has always been loosened,
enabling minds to become disillusioned.
A tender movement through love and light
ready to embrace you with all His might.
No need to take to fright, flight or fight,
because it is all going to be all right.

Let the delight of memory
prevail and rise from all the hell.
When the agreement is remembered,
somber is lifted and in all clarity and certainty,
eyes behold the spiritual blessings
that has always been gifted.

Then, you recall the fabrication of all worlds
and the factual world you have always known.
Deep down inside,
we know that Earth is a false kingdom
and everything on it,
including humans are illusion.

Why?

Because it all withers, rusts and turns to dust.
This is why we say, *In God, we trust*.
Willingness to remember the agreement
and their call of forgiveness permits kindness,
humbleness, patience and peace to enter
and they do become your center.
Through the sovereignty of Christ invested in us,
we tenderly thrust what is not of us.
We embrace the reality of who we truly are,
the spirit of love and light.

If you wish to remain in fear and darkness,
it is your prerogative.
However, when your time arrives for your miracle to enter,
celestial correction and healing is unavoidable.
This is where we find true freedom
from worlds of simulation preprogrammed
to dictate everything we think, say and do.
No longer be a fool and receive wisdom
and understanding of the gifts Christ enters with
and lays at your feet—

gifts that are so outstanding,
they permit the mind to expand
beyond passed flesh and bones.
Here, we learn to sing to the rhythm of holy tunes.
Remembering, we are all homies
from Heaven, our true haven.

Be brazen in all you think, say and do.
Utilize the holy, wholly wholesomeness
and you invite faith, humbleness, kindness,
peacefulness and patience to enter.
This summons love and light
who enters with wisdom and understanding.
Faith always follows
and the puzzle of where and how it all began
comes together again.
Remembrance of Alpha and Omega enters
and you breathe a sigh of relief
knowing what the people on earth truly need.
The biggest problem on earth lies within.
Reach for it and let the journey
of purification and cleansing begin.
This is a boomerang enabling the domino effect
to detect every mind willing to receive.

Positive energy outshines negative forces.
When we emanate this energy,
it goes to the universe and this is where
the boomerang becomes a reality.
When it hits the fabric of the universe,
it illuminates and the universe boomerangs
and it becomes a holy domino effect.

Be wise to elect
what truly must be addressed
and we can fix the world's biggest problems.

Keep in mind it all begins inside
as we are all the same in this world of merciless games.
Be willing to no longer permit ego thinking
to prevail and let God lift the veil of blindness
and ignorance to ruthless laws and agreements.
Bottom line, it is your choice to listen
to the voice of divinity,
to no longer roam in the fear and darkness
of vanity on earth and on any other worlds
that we inevitably traverse throughout the universe.

The universe was made
so we all have the chance to be born
into illusional worlds to experience what we are not.
We all agreed to every prewritten and premade worlds
and episodes that we ourselves wrote, designed and made.
Remember, we agreed to it one to another
before we were even born into it.
This is why forgiveness is inevitable,
my lovely brothers and sisters from Heaven.

Universe Whirlpools

Spiral deep into the chasm of universal whirlpools.
It has already been done, but no one remembers.

In the month of December,
Christ is praised never asking Him what it means
to be out in the suction of universe whirlpools.
We ask the very minds that do not know
then wonder why the dust gets blown.

In the dust is the devil of confusion,
hatefulness, bitterness and hostility,
and the meaning of divinity is lost.
Mind titter totters spins around
losing our minds just to spiral deeper down
universe whirlpools stuck in its black pool,
dazed, feeling like a fool.
This is not so cool!
It's like a day of April Fool's.
There is a golden rule in what we teach
but this does not mean, immediately,
that minds will get it and eyes will see.

Everyone is in pre-school,
this is why the majority of ego minds rule.

Even when the typhoon comes through,
many still look at things from the world's point of view.
Those who kneel and confess—
Christ is real—get the clue;
a moment of traversing into quantum immortality
safely escaping all of the brutality.

Universe whirlpools are for those who elect
to remain in the bondages of being a complete fool.
Christ love and light tenderly trickles in
outshining the black pool where the soul screams
to be redeemed safely in the hands of holiness.

The ultimate salvation is Christ adoration
that pulls every soul out of universe whirlpools.

The Separation

O, how could we ever have wanted
to live in a kingdom that would be inevitably undesirable?

A world where we would find
savage depression deep in the agonies of troubles.
The excitement of the unknown
must have been so overwhelming.
There comes a time
when we behold the significance
of separation and restoration into unification.
Separation is what caused
the birth into illusional worlds to dwell
where we thought it would be
fine, dandy and swell
but the separation began in the desperation
to know the opposite of love where there was none.
We coveted a force we had to make and called it fear
knowing it would turn out not to be so dear.
Here is where we find ourselves in tears,
when experiencing fear crystal clear.

Let us now steer far away
from what seems desirable
and bring the separation back to unification
under the shroud of love and light.
It would be wise to never again agree
to consume ourselves with such a decree
in the desperation to uncover
the discovery of what fear would bring
through our own making.
We forgot that love is what we are
and love is what we want.

Therefore, love is where we will return to
under the wings of God's embrace.

Here, there are no confusions, illusions or dreams,
only true reality in the Kingdom of stability,
holy exclusively where there are no borders.
In this Kingdom, we live life
in true freedom and never in boredom.
The separation is the beginning of depression
because we opted to leave God and Heaven.

We can incorporate to never again separate
from the elegance of His love, light, life and truth,
the essence of spirituality and Heaven.

Veil of Stardust

We are the co-makers of temporal being,
we are the co-creators of eternal life,
we mixed in with pleasure and strife.

We live and grow with the flow of the universe
and with a blow of stardust,
it clings to earth's crust.
Living and roaming since godzillions ago
as long as the universe epochs,
this seems forever as we traverse through
its galaxies of nights and more nights.

From the beginning of its explosions
to the black holes suction
is a process to salvage the old.
A course anew of time of life
in the cosmic formations.
We live under the veil of stardust
Always changing, constantly growing,
born into this world, born into that world
changing and exchanging this form
for the one born into the next.
A temporal part of an eternal creation,

An exemplary piece to divine revelation
where we can choose reincarnation.
A mind boggling thought
because we simply forgot all that we begot.
There is nothing we bought
in everything we made.
There is nothing naughty
no matter how fraughty.

The world from which we come
is where everything is given freely
and this is merely what we are to remember
in order to be enlighten to what truly matters.
The glisten of true stardust never remains dim
because truly, there is no sin.

No longer be scattered under the veil of stardust.
Rise and transform to the stretching of your essence.

The Reflection of the Stars

O, Father in Heaven, where is your spark?

I cannot behold the glistening
of the stars upon the sky of night
obscuring the stars of light.
My heart beats in fear as the storm
becomes awesome, lightning brightening,
thunder pounding, winds blowing, rain pouring,
splashing on the pavement ground.
I am barefoot'n, wearing my sheer white gown
as I stand with a bittersweet frown.
Drapes drawn, as if it were sunny at dawn.
At the wide open door,
leaves twirl on the hardwood floor.
I dance my way under the veil of rain
gazing upon the darkened sky.
Heart pounds as I ponder,
where the twinkle of your stars are.
In this moment of wonder,
I hear His tender whisper,
"The star lights are concealed by a thick dark mist,
so thick that the brightness of the stars
cannot penetrate the darkness of your mind and heart".

I sense a dark and heavy cloud follow me
wherever I prance about as I dance my way through
the hardwood floor to the door.
O Father, let it be I am free in readiness
to let go of the darkness in my heart.
I no longer wish to let it bind and blind me deeper
into the pit of darkness of self-deception.

I wish your light shines upon and through me.
Let the eerie blackness lift from my mind and heart
so I may be a witness to the light upon the stars.
Every soul within is a bright shining star.
My heart's desire is to be a witness
to the light in me and the light in them.

Let the rays of light drizzle through
the fabric of the blackness of night.
Let it tenderly burst through the darkness
of the minds who behave as cruel as fools.
Let us behold in all clarity and certainty
the twinkle of light eager to shine upon
and through the darkness
of troubled minds and hearts.

O Father, let the light rays be full-blown
as we remember you have always known us
and we have always known you.
Through my willingness to behold and embrace
the light in my brothers, the stars glisten
through the darkness of the sky.
In glee, I gracefully dance and prance
About the hardwood floor to the door
and past its threshold.

Barefoot'n, as if in the days of my childhood
onto the wet pavement of the cool cement,
I am a witness to the dark sky
full of glistening star lights
glowing its divine dazzle ever so bright.

The light within is fully lit,
now a witness to the spirit's lift.
Such a glorious gift to be an eyewitness
to the reflection of the shining stars we all are.

Such a lovely oneness of glistening brightness,
for we are the reflection of the stars
ever so close to the spark inside.

O Father, let us live in you,
I no longer fear the mighty storm.
I understand that lightning is symbolic,
a reminder to embrace the Spirit
where we are witness to the reflection
of everyone's bright shining star inside.
The roaring thunder is emblematic.
O, how ecstatic I am to know the darkness
within has never been anyone's eternal twin.

O holy brothers, do not let the chaotic mess
deafen the hearing to the voice of the Holy Spirit.
Let us be a witness to the radiance within
and opt to know the holy reflection
of Christ in all His glory.
Rain washes away all the bittersweet,
heart does not skip a beat.
Let it renew loveless to loving,
sadness to happiness and war to peace.
Let the cleansing and purification begin
wiping out the madness within,
the ego's crazy thoughts of bleakness.

In togetherness, willingness is the light
that carries the Spirit through its stages of storms
where it is a witness to the reflection
of the lovely face of Christ inside.
The darkened storms within
have no power, let's not cower.

Let the beam of light whisk away
the devastating darkness that cannot forever rule.
Let it purify the sickness of mind,
bringing union to the Kingdom of calmness
where we realize God is
the love and light within
and we are not to fear.

He is the brilliance of innocence
in every soul on earth and throughout the universe
as we traverse into galaxies most devastating.
The stars reflect upon the mind as a reminder,
that we are the reflection of He who is within.
The reflection of the stars is us
because we are God's bright, diamond super stars
no matter the storms that whisk up
in the mind and heart.
They are synthetic and pathetic ways of sickness
within our puny psychedelic thoughts.

We enter our minds' wellness at the time appointed,
restoring the split mind to holy, wholly, wholesomeness.

Clash of Blues

On Earth and in the universe,
everything we clash into brings trauma, pain and sorrow.

Through spiritual vision, we behold and know
the truth from the false in every aspect of life
on earth, the universe and Heaven.
Earth shaking, mountains exploding,
buildings crumbling, cars crashing,
streets collapsing, dirt sinking, mud sliding,
ice melting, seas flooding, heat overwhelming
and everyone yelling.
Universe upholding hellish worlds,
burning stars, moons of calamity,
pulsating star light, darkened moonlight,
galaxies galore and much more.
This is just a glimpse of the fleet
that dream worlds offer.

In Heaven, everything is completely wide open
that nothing ever runs into each other.
Even if it did, everything zooms right through each other
tenderly embracing one another in a dance of love.
In Heaven, there are no such things
as explosions, crumbling, clashing and collapsing.
Everything is so perfect,
there are no such things as accidents, trauma
or tears of fear and pains of sorrow.
There is nothing to toss
and there is certainly no loss.

Everything in Heaven
is tightly, tenderly and perfectly braided
that nothing ever falls apart.

It is the royal, holy glistening golden white vine
that is forever divinely intertwined.
It never tangles, mangles, crumbles, clashes or collapses
because it is an open golden glistening white vine
that is magnificently true and kind.

Everything of God
is freedom of life, forever alive
and this we can look forward to
when we learn to walk forward and skyward
through the brilliant quantum leap of spiritual vision.

We are witnesses
to the evidence of conflicting dreadfulness
on earth and in the universe—
such dreams are nonexistent in Heaven.

Heaven is true, for there is no such thing
as a clash of blues.

Purple Sky World

Into a world with purple skies,
where one can breathe just fine.

It is a dazzling depth of pink auras,
a spectacular chorus aglow
with golden stars afloat
and white crows expose.

It is not a plasma painting
and will not leave one fainting.
The crunchy chirping of gold doves above,
bring the senses to passionate love.
Such a view to behold,
like a white sky glistening gold.
The purple skies take ahold
with white and gold birds in the fold.

It is a Kingdom of extreme exploration
but brings about a thrilling elation.
The purple sky can seem like haunting hazel
but the melody of harps
gloriously transports harmonious music
to the heart.

This does not bring a bitter taste of tart,
for its magnificent resonance abolishes all arrogance—
a string of elegance on this world of wondrous elements
where there is nothing menacing.
There is nothing unstylish about it,
for its superb classiness brings utter happiness.

The purple sky world
is a kingdom of relevance.

Black Hole

A recycle machine that is majestically powerful in its suction,
a force of its own source.

It would not be in existence
without everything else
the universe upholds,
including us.

They are powerful recycle machines,
yet they are not a clunk of metal
that rusts and settles.
It does not run on fuel,
it sustains itself by its own duel of sovereignty
that eventually turns on itself
just like everything else in dream worlds.

Before its lifespan runs out,
the power in its recycle phase is immense.
It cleans up all the universal debris
during its recycle spree
and this has always been since time began

A black hole is a merciless force
but it is also a merciful point of source
because though its suction is powerful,
there comes a time when it also reverses its force
and something extraordinary
and majestic happens in that moment.

It can be a tuning of communication
if we just learn to remember
how to master telepathic communication
through divine meditation.

We are the transmitters,
no matter the distance of all existence.

During its recycle phase,
it certainly looks merciless
while we are witnesses to it
devouring everything that enters
the point of its threshold
seeming like the elements
reached the point of no return.

This illusion is deceiving because
it also becomes a merciful machine.
Everything it recycles
are made anew.
Nothing goes to waste during its brew
and when its ready to spew,
it does not do so
like a champagne corkscrew.
Its merciful phase is so tender
that it is such a majestic event to witness.

There comes a time when its suction
completely stops its destruction
and this is where it becomes a majestic force
because it reverses its suction.
This is where something extraordinary happens
and it can be very eerie,
but so fascinating and cheery!
Have you ever blown bubbles
from a plastic bottle
filled with water and soap?

We've probably already seen a bubble
tenderly emerge from another bubble.
This is the same scenario a black hole goes through
during its phase of a celestial aerial.

In this atonement of a black hole,
everything becomes extremely still and silent
and its tender gravity permits its reversal
to gently spew out other worlds
into universes, including our own.

This is where everything we spiritually behold
is truly majestic!
This is where the Holy Spirit
gently hurdles you through quantum leap
where you enable yourself to see
and remember everything
you have always known
because you created it along
with all the Sonship.
It's an imperial trip!
We just forgot all that we begot.
Scientists call the threshold of a black hole,
general relativity, an event horizon.

The period of the black holes' sneaky lure,
through illusional physics, this is what we witness.
At the point of the black holes' decency
is where quantum leap enters
if you so wish to permit yourself to travel through it
with the guidance of the Holy Spirit,
for God is the authority of quantum leap.
This is why we never find it
because we seek it through illusional physics,
meaning, we are looking for it
outside of our own thought schmooze
where we snooze.

Through the eyes of "layman terms",
this is what we see,
enabling ourselves to remain blind
until we permit ourselves to behold
through the eyes of spiritual vision
where we enable ourselves to perceive
through the perception of the Holy Spirit.
He shows us everything that looks ruthless
is not all that merciless all the time,
for even we have moods of cruelty and decency.

A black hole looks merciless
at its phase of suction but it is merciful at its majestic phase,
its point of its reversal
because in that moment of stillness and silence,
it begins its tender evacuation,
returning everything it spews anew
back into illusional realities.
This is the evidence
that there is no such thing as,
points of no return.

Black holes recycle everything only to be renewed again,
restarting the illusional life cycle all over again.
But when will it all end?

Echoing Thunder

Echoing thunder, a force not seen,
like the queen bee we never see.

During winter season,
ears are witness to the divine sovereignty
of echoing thunder from above
the sphere of the sun.

At the listening of its roaring rumble,
its vibrating sound is so striking,
it makes one jump from off the couch,
feet planted to the ground.
Hoops and haulers of hallelujah
shriek through the room
in honor of its powerful sound
as my heart pounds in anticipation
to witness its sonic source of vibration.
Such a roaring force is exciting,
not boring nor frightening.

Its sonic echoing thunder
sent me on a journey of exploring its source of origin.
Then, I remembered the day and hour
I asked God to let me hear
the divine sonic power of His voice,
let me witness the nature of its sonic source.

Lo and behold, through the gray clouds
of dimness, without grimness,
He showed me a spiral of His source.
At the sonic moment of His echoing thunder,
I am witness to the divine power
at the center of the spiral.

The force of a burst of sonic energy
blasts cleverly and tenderly
as my eyes gaze upon it.
The sonic sound and its vibration
is the glory of echoing thunder
discharging from the center of an invisible spiral
that God has granted me
to emerge from optical illusion to spiritual vision.

I instinctively know it is symbolic
to the loving, tender and peaceful voice of eternity,
our Father in Heaven.
Some fear it,
yet there is no need to
as it is best to embrace
and get to know it.

He is a God of mercy and grace,
the sovereignty of His booming, sonic sounds of thunder.

Hellish Worlds

Earth's Milky Way houses hellish worlds,
yet as we venture out, we become witness to more hellish worlds.

We seek Heaven
as we travel deeper into outer space.
We are onlookers to the harshness
of various hellish worlds we made.
We travel zillions of light years away
from our own Milky Way.
We still have not reached the glorious natural light
of the glistening golden world of Heaven.
We started the galactic travels
fresh, eager and hopeful,
but find we are worn, subdued and hopeless
through the voyage taken.

We grow tired, sad, disheveled,
dispirited and dejected
from dodging asteroids, comets, speeding pebbles,
fearsome movements, frightening figures,
and the strange and bizarre gravity of hellish worlds.
We started fresh zillions of light years ago
Seeking Heaven outward until we finally come
to our divine senses to search inward.
There is a universe within where we find Heaven
because we are the love and light
of the glistening golden Heavenly Kingdom
that is alive and well,
thriving in abundant life authentic.
All this time, we traveled the night of the universe,
we thought this was outside of us.

To learn it is inside, is to behold
all that we want to know.

This is where we remember
how to build spaceships that permit us
to traverse the universe we think
is on the outside of us.
To discover it is within is the twist.
Godzillions ago,
we kept ourselves imprisoned in the darkness
where we remain blind to the light inside
where we behold everything.

Only through willingness to see through spiritual vision
can our light outshine the darkness.
All it takes is an invitation to the Holy Spirit
to light the dimness within
and we behold right through the night
we uphold through ignorance.
Through God's perspective, darkness dissipates
and we do not hesitate to gaze our eyes
upon the glistening golden world of Heaven
that outshines all of the hellish worlds in the universe
of our own synthetic and pathetic madness.

We recognize we have been gone
from Heaven for so long,
we spend lifetimes seeking home.
To feel lost and alone in dream and hellish worlds
is to want to lay down and curl up,
wondering if we will ever escape underworlds.
This is where we come to the realization that
barren hellish worlds are worlds
we occupied and utilized godzillions ago.

Their life span and our own
has come to its end godzillion times over,
only to be replenished and rebirthed into it
again and again only to occupy and be a slave
to the wrathful god we made.

When we do enter the realization of the point of return,
we go back to earth's Milky Way to tell the tale
that earth's travelers no longer traverse
the darkness of the universe outward
because the lesson here is
to learn to know of it inward.

The light of Heaven in us
outshines the darkness, not of us
where we uphold spiritual vision
in all clarity and certainty
that we finally found Heaven inside.
Here, we remember all the hellish worlds
we are witnesses too
are but ancient ruins that once were alive
and thriving with an abundant life as we know it
and various life forms we have forgotten.

Barren hellish worlds were replenished,
time and time again to be recycled godzillion times over
from godzillions ago where we behold the illusion
of all its wreckage as they suspend
in the vast of universes darkness.

Yet, we can escape it.

Plumas National Forest

Bright sunrays beam
through rustic autumn leaf-filled trees.

Autumn pine aroma fills the air,
a breathing climate I can bear.
Driving through winding roads,
tiny squirrels swiftly cross,
so happy it is at no loss.

Pointed green pine trees at cliff's edge
standing tall congregating
at mountaintops and mountainsides.
Bright yellow colorful leaf filled trees,
a breathtaking sight to see.

Hiking through the Pacific Crest Trail
was an almighty shout of hail.
Lush greenery thickets on the forest floor
has no limits.
While soaring overhead,
I hear a screeching, echoing wild hawk call.
A scream of *kee-eeeee-arr*.
Free flowing freshwater captures my attention,
a glorious sound of wonder.
Ponds in various areas of the trail
is a delightful moment of bonding
with every water particle.

Hiked alone deep into Plumas National Forest
and friends asked, "Weren't you afraid?"
"No, I knew in my heart God was with me
with every step I took.

Through my faith, I did nothing more than trust in Him
where I bathed in His peace
through this forest journey,"
was my reply.

It is a glorious wonder when we know in certainty
that God is with us everywhere we go.
We can literally feel His holy presence
when we elect to connect.
On an autumn day at Plumas National Forest,
I heed to my calling on the day and hour
of this season for a glorious reason.

Everything went as perfect
as I expected it to be
because I permitted my mind, heart and spirit
to be aligned with divinity.
It was such a majestic event
that to this day, I cherish and remember it
like it was three minutes ago.

Bright sunrays beam
through rustic autumn leaf-filled trees.

Divinity

The ego is strange and bizarre,
a puny god we made.

When we are willing to admit to this
is when God permits His Holy Spirit
to take us through quantum leap
into the love and light of divinity.

Divinity is the holiness
within each and every one of us,
regardless of all the hurtful and brutal things
we think, say and do.
This is why we must be careful
about specialness because specialness
separates us, whereas holiness unites us.

Unification is a quantum leap
into love, light, life and truth—
the essence of joyfulness, peacefulness, humbleness,
kindness, forgiveness, patience, faith, hope,
freedom, unity, safety, generosity and royalty.
They are celestial holy qualities
that bring us out of the strange and bizarre world
of the ego's sinister prison in the network of the mind.

Do not despair, for the Holy Spirit is here.
God authorizes Him to tenderly hurtle you
into the Kingdom of true naturalism
and realism of the loveliness
within each and every one of us.

Under the veil of love and light
is when we are free to be
where we see the celestial wonders under the openness
of Heaven's sunlight where truth prevails.
Our lovely spirit always remembers
the divine qualities inside each and every one of us.
This is why the Spirit leaps with joy when it hears truth.

Willingness to gaze upon
the bright and beautiful views of Heaven
and the divine whiteness
with golden glistening clouds
is the divinity of who you are
and where you are from.
Remembering immortality has been around
since eternity to the end of time
in all its glory where we thrive
in love, joy peace and royalty.

Embrace the immortality of eternity,
for it is your inheritance of divinity.

Self-Born

A glistening golden light
in the midst of pure cleanliness.

A virgin sea of blackness
in the open space of emptiness,
He breathed in His aroma of fresh energy,
a scent ever so warm and cozy
like a newborn baby.
It sparked the shimmer of golden light
to be self-born in pure delight
of His sparkly golden light
of uncontaminated adoration.

A glistening golden light is pure in its bright sight,
all joyful to be energy-born to transform
into the God He is and will forever be.
A whirlwind of the holiness ordained
the pureness of oceans' blackness of liveliness
to be His Kingdom He calls Heaven.
His glisten golden presence is magnetic energy
so extraordinary it attracts the black ocean of vigor
to His pure, clean and fresh aroma of everything majestic
He is self-created to be.

From the core of His mind, heart and spirit,
His tender mesmeric storm influenced
your holiness to be free to form
in the gentle breeze of charismatic energy.

A magnetism ever so germ free and charming,
there was nothing alarming about being self-born
into the God He is who would be
the godzillion number superseding
all numbers forevermore.

He is our darling Father in Heaven
guarding the pure and sparkly open sea of purity,
like a white winged starling
that is so enchantingly advancing.
He is self-born to bring divine life to the open space
of fascinating energy of blackness.
But even at His advancement,
His glistening golden light remains
the foundation of who He truly is forevermore.
He is the essence of divinity, infinity
and created the Trinity to be
His holy and royal family endlessly.
For the open space of blackness,
He ordained it with His love and light of whiteness,
which is infinite and this is where
He creates His Heavenly Kingdom.

God is self-born
from a glistening golden light of pure energy
expanding His mind and spirit
of divine holy, wholly, wholesomeness.
He is a God of love, joy, peace, clarity,
certainty, safety, purity, unity and royalty,
the essence of love, light, life and truth.

This is why He is the one and only true God
who is the security blanket of all creation, forevermore.

A glistening golden light
in the midst of pure cleanliness.

Glistening White Vine

The vast opening of loveliness is pure brightness,
a liveliness of lightness, still in calmness, the essence of holiness.

As God emerges His light into darkness,
it gently enters its starkness.
His light lovingly, calmly and tenderly
drapes the blackness.
In love, light and calmness,
He embraces the darkness
for it is ever so serene, pure and clean
with not a speck of
meanness, cruelness and maliciousness.
Through His love and light,
He elects to make the dark and stark space
His foundation for His Heavenly Kingdom
He would create.
When He finishes creating part of Heaven,
He decides He would no longer be alone.
Through His thoughtful words of beauty,
He commences to clone His holy and royal family
around the glistening golden circle
of love, light, life and truth,
which is the essence of His
Holiness, Spirit, Heaven and Eternity.

In honor of His creation,
He manifests a glistening golden white vine
as a memoir to every soul,
forever intertwined with His holy, royal
golden seal of love and light.
The glistening golden white vine
is forever anchored in the garden of enlightenment
safely in the Kingdom of Heaven.

At your willingness to recall your Kingdom,
His Holy Spirit tenderly guides you
through quantum leap into the past of His creation
where you become a witness
to every beautification He ever created.

The glistening golden white vine
is a memoir of God's holy mind, spirit
and your own forever tightly and tenderly interlaced
and this you can never escape.

When you become witness through spiritual vision,
you relearn to embrace what you would not want to escape anyway.

Sweet Healing

Let your thoughts intertwine like a growing glistening white vine with the Mind of Holiness, for this is utter sweetness.

Be willing to allow His sweet healing
be like silky golden honey swirling atop
a glisten golden white milky cloud
where you are witness to its sheer delight.

Take in its aroma, taste it, meditate it
and let it bring sweet healing
to the vine of your mind
intertwined with God's mind.

No matter where you search for the healing
of corrupt thinking, go deeper in search of it
and you will inevitably find
love and light at the center of it.
In your perseverance to escape the darkness,
the love and lightness of His Holiness
tenderly draws nearer and nearer to you.

The adoration of His sweet healing
glorifies the growing, glistening golden
white vine of your mind.
As it intertwines skyward,
it escapes the darkness of space
reaching the glistening golden white clouds
of Heaven.

The sweet healing to our precious minds
tenderly ensures we remain
on the glistening golden white vine
of the salvation of our minds.

You are the spark of the golden white vine
tightly braided with God's mind we all inevitably find.

The Dreamer and the Dream

You do not recognize that to look within,
you have the power to make a holy detour.

The deep sleep has taken you
to an ancient ground of dreams
where the ego dictates your every move
leading you to a rebound
of an unpleasant demise.

The ego tells you to look outward not inward
but there is nothing outside of your view,
only inside of you.

It brings fear upon you and tells you
if you look inside of yourself,
you see the sinful self.

Yet, there is no sin in you
but it is the ego who lies in wait within
and does not want you to notice
its sinful and hateful plots,
the sickening ways of its dictations.
It is the dreamer and the dream you made,
ensuring no memory to the ego's ancient sin
that you asked it to dictate
ensuring you are its puppet.

You are pure, clean and sinless
but wondered what it would be like
to be tainted, filthy and sinful.
So separation from holiness and sinlessness
transformed cleanliness to filthiness,
casting yourself from true reality to a dream.

Here, you became the dreamer and the dream,
planting yourself in the egos sinful schemes
making you fearful to look inward
because it does not want you
to behold the love, light, life
and truth in you.

As the dreamer and the dream,
to behold and know
the glistening golden circle of holiness,
abolishes the belief you are sinful.
To grasp the love in you
closes down the tremble of fear
not of you.
To notice you are light,
outshines the dark.
To know you are joy,
stops the ploy of sadness.
To discern that you are sinless
ends guiltiness
and to recognize you are peace,
stops the idea of war.

Here, you break free from the bondage of chains
and shackles of the ego's sinister prison
to soar into the bliss of holy freedom.

The divine power invested
in the dreamer and the dream
shatters the dimension of sinful, fearful feats
and its tender suction gently pulls you inward
into the reality of the holy, lovely light
of sinlessness, guiltlessness, joyfulness
and peaceful Kingdom you know all too well.

Here, you are happy to remember
the dreamer and the dream is an illusion
and that Heaven is the conclusion
of the ancient sinful, fearful experiences
you finally spiritually wakeup from
to return home to your natural state
of holiness, wholeness and wholesomeness—
the epitome of devoutness.

The dreamer and the dream you made
to fake sinful and fearful deeds
are realities you will clearly be happy to see
are pointless, meaningless and senseless ideas
because in the end, in certitude,
you will behold it is truly fake, indeed.

You do not recognize that to look within,
you have the power to make a holy detour.

How to Wake From the Dream

Waking from the dream can be done anywhere
and at any time one chooses to do so.

It can even be done in your own home.

If you choose to do this in your home,
begin in a calm state of mind
and in a quiet small space
so as to not displace the focus needed
and you don't become confused or heated.

Get cozy and comfy,
slowly and tenderly look at every object
in the small space of the room
and recognize your attachment
and lovingly detach yourself from them.

Repeat this as many times needed
so you are not defeated.
Be willing,
for this will be fulfilling.

When you are ready be steady
and take your focus
to a larger room in your home.

When you have completed the focus
to disconnect from the objects in your home,
turn your focus outward.

In your mind's eye,
gradually and softly take your focus
to look upon the trees and leaves,
grass and trash, cars and parks,
fences and hedges, pastures and grasses,
weeds and streets, wildflowers and plants,
mountains and fountains, oceans and seas
and houses and buildings.

Focus your connection to these things,
then gently refocus disconnection
of all these things.

It is ever so pleasing to be released
from the connection to the objects
because the disconnection
is a glory of contentment.
Breathe steady and firmly but gently
and you will fly like a birdie out of the dream
and into a world smitten with glee.

Return gently and be mindful
that you are not surprised
to find yourself extremely relaxed and friendly
when you have done this correctly.

This is how to wake from the dream
in all its fulfillment.

The Only Law There Is

The laws of man will cease,
but the law of God is the only law there is—
celestial and eternal.

Live comfortably in this world of illusional dreams
and remain in righteousness in all your ways.
Do not break meaningless laws,
keep your non-righteous ways at bay
for the ego minds certainly flay you around
and bind you to evil games of their own.
However, in ruthless worlds of thinking,
sometimes even those who abide
are broadside and dried out to hang.

Just because someone points the finger
and accuses another does not make it so.
How easily we believe what others say
because we do not keep
our own sick thinking at bay.
Keep your mind healthy and listen
to the soft peaceful voice in you
to bind your virtuous ways
with God's meaningful laws of
forgiveness and redemption.
Meaningless laws are crazy ideas,
a harsh reality of a sick mentality
that will not last forever.

The meaningful laws of God frees you
and enables you to spree in love forever.
It is always best to bind your ways
in the laws of God's love and light.

It is possible to do in a world of sickness
but you must be willing to listen
to the voice of the Holy Spirit's guidance
who never brings about frightening things.

If He does, it is brief
and only to get a point across.
His comfort and the peace of Christ always follows.
Patience is a virtue because we live
in a world of time,
therefore, everything takes time
for wisdom and understanding to enter.
Time and timelessness are in the mind
but time is illusion and timelessness is realism
yet you can gain all the gifts of eternity in time.

This is not a warped perception,
this is the clarity of spiritual vision,
a quantum leap into a peek of infinity.
Forgive the crazy laws we make
and recognize they are only fake.
Be willing to embrace the laws of
love, light, forgiveness and redemption
and let yourself be as free as a bird.
Be of good cheer when you come to a swerved curve
and remember that joy and peace
is what you and the Sonship deserve.
We propped the curves only to live it
because we wanted to experience it.
Indeed, to uphold this in our memory
brings comfort and joy.
This is a moment in time
where we look at each other
eye to eye and chuckle
and the intense buckle of strongholds are released.

The remembrance of all we have ever known
comes through our own spiritual experiences
where love, light, life and truth enters.
This is where we are showered with peace,
which supersedes the reality of something different
that we wanted to know.

Remember the laws of love,
for it leads you to the golden road of Heaven,
you and your brothers are worthy of.

The only law there is, is the law of God's Love
that frees you because freedom
into love, light, life and truth
is most certainly your royal inheritance.

Blind Dreamer

A blind dreamer has not yet awakened
to the reality of bittersweet experiences.

Through spiritual awakening,
a blind dreamer beholds the meaninglessness attraction
of world events and hears its voices of sad stories.
Words of heartbreak is all that's muttered
on a world so cluttered with chaotic senselessness.
Behold the worthlessness
in the illusion of the world
and in the actions of the wicked
that are merely self-deception.
All the dangers are reflections of events
that have already come and gone.

This is where one prepares to rise
to the reality that all the worldly enticement
and its sad voices are merely illusion.
At spiritual awakening,
a blind dreamer gets extremely bored
of living in the dreadful dream.
A blind dreamer no longer has the desire
to receive what the cluttered world offers.
At full spiritual awakening,
the only thing a blind dreamer finds interesting
is sharing the testament
of what God's Holy Spirit has shown
when the truth of God, Heaven
and everything else prevails.

A blind dreamer's hand rises to the chest
only to ask to let the heart no longer be torn
through the duration as a wanderer
on a world of ferocious storms.

The dreamers do not recognize they are asleep,
thinking they are awake.
When dreamers involve themselves
in the dramatization of worldly events,
they are asleep and dreaming.
When dreamers involve themselves
in love, joy, peace, kindness,
humbleness, patience and faith,
they are awake, indulging into the truth
of the past, present and future realities inside.

A blind dreamer patiently awaits for God
to pluck the inner boredom
of all the outrageous and radical quorums.
A blind dreamer asks to bless
the mess in all minds and hearts
with meaningful excitement
to enlighten minds frighten.
Among all the drama, there is useful cheer
without the useless fear to enable God's message
of every holy and orderly lessons
every dreamer seeks to bear.
Every dreamer inevitably stops in steadiness
for the readiness of holy sanctification
as God would have it be.

In holy stillness, dreamers complete their mission
of God's vision and their own.
Through spiritual awakening,
a blind dreamer is blind no more.
This is why one is bored
until the boredom is lifted and the spirit rises
into the Heavenly stream of holiness
and the blind dreamer is ready
to heed God's calling,
offering undivided attention to the mission.

The blind dreamer who is blind no more
asks God to move forward in the steps
they willed together before the blind dreamer
was even born into global disasters
and pleas to let the weathered boredom be gone
because the blind dreamer who is blind no more
is done with world chaos.

A blind dreamer has not yet awakened
to the reality of bittersweet experiences.

Heaven

We have forgotten, Heaven is our haven.

We are not so brazen to recall this
but through willingness,
we can regain its memory.
Heaven is so pure, clean and fresh
because there is no such thing as flesh.
It is the spirit that lives
in the glorious Kingdom of Heaven
where every life form
thrives in love, joy and peace.

From microscopic life to alien life forms,
we all dwell in unification and freedom
where there is no such thing
as any kind of irritation.
The Spirit freely sprees everywhere
it wishes to go without any passports and keys
because there are no borders, locks and doors.

I was ever so floored
when faith took me further into Heaven
reminding me of all its beauty.
I flew in awe to the wonders of Heaven
where there are no such thing as flaws.
Trees, plants and flowers greet in angelic hymns
the joy to convoy the attraction
to the magnificence of Heaven.

Faith escorts me over the trees and beyond.
I look upon glistening golden roads
where everyone walks barefoot.

As we soar over the golden streets,
she shows me gorgeous colors of pastures
where I hear the hymns of their violin blades
as we approach celestial everglades.

Mountain tops are so vast
and there is no need to ask, Why?
Because instinctively we know
this is the nature of Heaven
and that this has always been.
Glorious colors can be seen from up yonder
and there are no words to describe
the realism that is beyond imagination.
As much as I would love to be more descriptive,
again, there are no words to describe Heaven.

We have forgotten, Heaven is our haven.

Get Past the Darkness of Murkiness

I cannot see through the murkiness of the sea
where the light does not shine.

As I become aware
I am in the deepest part of the ocean,
the fog of its blackness thickens.
Deep beneath its plane,
I cannot breath.
I zoom to the sea's surface in a panic.
as a trickle of light rays penetrate
through the sea's sparkly particles.

Approaching closer to sea's surface,
I begin to notice they are sunrays.
Like a buoy,
my head rises above sea's plane.
I take a deep breath,
nice to escape sea's murkiness.
I see a body of water all around me,
pure joy engulfs me
because you see, I breathe the sigh of life
when I thought I was about to die.
I gaze upon the blue sky
and indulge the sunlight.
Its rays are short lived.
Sunlight is cloaked by a cloud of darkness
that glides through airs current,
it shadows over me.

An emotion of fear drowns my peace
as if the black clouds goal is to devour me.

It's ironic, I get past the murkiness
of darkness at the bottom of the sea,
but now this dreariness of a cloud
reminds me of the dark thick cloud inside me
that follows me everywhere I go.
O Father, how can I get past the darkness
of murkiness of the cloud over me
as I remain buoyant upon the sea?

I humbly plea, O Father in Heaven,
let your rays of light outshine this cloud of darkness
so I may see past what I must get through inside me.
Let me be bold and behold through vertical eyes
how to get past the black cloud in fearlessness.
I want to live in peace,
let it befall me as this darkness
of murkiness surrounds me.

Our Father in Heaven says,
"Forgive it and it shall flee."
I close my eyes,
bow my head and in silence,
I forgive it.

Stillness and calmness befalls me.
Indeed, the black cloud fades into nothingness.
Now I clearly see a city in front of me.
I feel sand beneath my feet,
I instinctively know,
whilst in the midst of the black cloud,
I am holy towed to the sea shore.
Of course, it is through forgiveness,
I get past the darkness of murkiness
in the depths of minds sea, I realize.

To bind myself to the physical world,
I had blinded myself to the spiritual world.

Blindness spears me
to the darkness of murkiness that consumes me
drowning me in pains and sorrows,
not to life, but to death.
In this moment, my eyes open.
In faith, I turn
and dive back into the ocean.
As I gracefully torpedo
deeper and deeper into its abyss,
His light rays follow
lighting the way as clear as crystal.

Then I remember,
sunrays are not so powerful
to shine upon
the deepest part of oceans floor.
My heart leaps of joy
that God's light follows me.
At touchdown, I softly caress
white sands at the sea's floor.
Then, in a swim of dance,
I torpedo to the surface
to dance on the seashore.
Upon the white sands, I twirl and swirl
like a disco of light piercing
through my mind's murkiness.
I breathe the breath of life in peace
knowing I have control over darkness' deceit.
Under the glory of God's glisten,
I am no longer blind.
I behold the glory of His holy sovereignty,
now free to spree under the fullness
of His love and light in joy and peace.

This is Heaven,
the completeness of eternity
that reigns within me.
In all clarity and certainty
under the veil of His serenity,
I behold the richness of infinity
that sends me into a moment of serendipity,
enjoying my new found spirituality.
Now I see in all simplicity ,
the pleasantness of His elegance—
a kingdom where there is never any need
to balance or even face a challenge
because in the wide open skies of Heaven,
dark arts of wild dreams are non-existent.

It is only in illusion, I learned to get past
the darkness of murkiness through forgiveness.

Black Rain

In the genesis of dream worlds,
we made water worlds.

The holy instant holy water showered
upon the atmosphere of the universe,
it transformed from clear rain to black rain.
Water worlds once barren
now look like bubble membrane,
afloat in the midst of what was
a virgin sky of cleanliness.

Membranes travel to their appointed destinations
to be anchored where they suspend
and blend into the darkness of the universe.
We are its maker and gave the command
for supersonic thunder and lightning strikes
to commence upon water worlds.

Whirlwinds wisp through
upon the infancy of universes' movements.
As we give the command to each component to enter,
membranes explode throughout universes' movements
gliding speedily so as to avoid clustering.
Yet, wreckage and clutter is inevitable,
as they are symbolic to the havoc
we would witness and experience
at the appointed time given to be born
into dream worlds ready for human habitation.

It was a mesmerizing sight to behold
the infancy of housing the virgin sky
that would be transformed
from glorious to absolute eeriness.

A now surrealistic world
that would house synthetic puny worlds
that would mature to sustain human life
that we would birth into.

Here, we give the greatest performances
of the total opposite of what God and Heaven is,
but all it is are experiences of self-deception.

We left the glistening golden world of Heaven
to enter eerie, dreary worlds in the universe
that began with holy water
being transformed into black rain.
This ensures we all gain synthetic experiences
that dream worlds would offer.
In dream worlds, craziness prevails for a time.
The wrathful, puny god we made to worship
in dream worlds is a temporary ego network
that inevitably goes into oblivion.
By our own making,
it was brought into existence to rule
with a callous mind and an iron fist.
Keep in mind, there is no wrath in God.
It thrives on fear and darkness,
and as time goes on, it goes ballistic
in the rhythm of viciousness.

The veil of black rain brings fears and tears
we would all bear
even though there is nothing to fear
because God is always near.

Oh dear, be grateful the ego is a temporary god
we elected to experience.

To remember the agreement
is to recall all the polar molecules
we ourselves placed in black rain.
God is generous to let us house
hydrogen and oxygen atoms in every water droplet
to sustain life on dream worlds
through the duration of every life span
no matter the form.

We are born to roam illusional worlds
under the laws of God's freedom,
for He values every life form
born into dream worlds.

When the act of each play is over,
we return to God's glistening golden love and light
where we crossover because we made black rain
around God's glory to ensure
there really is no worry to every eerie dreamer.

*In the end, we return to being cheery because no one is forgotten
in the mind and heart of God.*

Child of Godzillion

Earth is a controlled environment
not for experiments,
but for experiences we asked to live out.

The body is a means of a prison we ourselves made
to house the spirit while we experience the fears of darkness
even though the spirit is also in Heaven.

The sun is not only a small portion of God's light
that suspends in the atmosphere of the universe
shining upon earth's skies.
It is a reminder to us
of God's loving and open light inside.

When we gaze upon the sky,
we are witnesses to the shining, burning sphere
of light God lends to sustain the temporal life
we are here to experience
and to behold all over the world of dreams
so we can awake from the blindness
of the things we left behind in Heaven.
Be happy we are not forever hurdled out
into complete darkness where there are
worlds of devastation
as far as our telescopes can see.
Worlds we ourselves made
that will destroy us.
In fact, just the dark gravity alone
will strangle us to death in the human sense.
Not to mention all of the spooky props
we ourselves buttressed to manifest in its time.

Be happy we were given the authorization
to miscreate a miniature imitation globe of Heaven
to be rebirthed time and time again
until we come to the divine realization
and acceptance that we are holy and sinless.
We are children of godzillion years old
whom God adorably loves.
We are ancient, but forever young and vibrant.
We are gorgeous and flawless spirits that never age,
a hair is never out of place, with impeccable skin
and never sick because this is the nature of spirit,
the essence of immortality.

Child of godzillion years old,
we are forever fresh, young and clean as God is
because His light never burns out
and neither does our own.

However, our light can grow dim
when we separate from Him and we did.
This is why we are out in the universe
until we come to rediscover
the holiness of love and light within.

God is the source of love and light,
the essence of holiness and sinlessness
and we are divinely connected
to the only love and light there is.

God is the core of everyone and everything.
This makes us children of godzillion years old.
He created us.
Godzillion can never be measured,
not through physical eyes
because it is the treasure measured
only through spiritual vision.

Willingness is all it takes
to let the Holy Spirit lead us into it
because it is a quantum leap
we cannot find or manifest alone.

He will fill up our cup
with spiritual knowledge and vision.
In the beginning,
He can only feed us breadcrumbs
because to bless us with
full spiritual knowledge and vision all at once
of God and godzillion will hurdle us
deeper into madness because our puny human mind
cannot wrap or grasp a godzillion number
that is beyond measure.

Child of godzillion,
we were created godzillions ago
in timelessness
and we can never measure this with time.
Until we accept the quantum leap journey
with the Holy Spirit into spiritual vision and knowledge,
we can never regain celestial memory swiftly.

It is only through spiritual vision
can you grasp and view the enormity of godzillion.

Spiritual Universal Hero

In every and any circumstance and situation,
He is always with us because never are we alone
in the universal field of fear and darkness.

It feels that we are alone, but the truth is,
we have a spiritual universal hero
that emerges from the Heavenly realm
to guide us through every dreadful experience.

We feel the immense strength of the spirit within
that wants nothing more than to survive and live
through horrific events and illnesses.
This is the evidence
that death goes against our true nature.

All we have ever known is eternal life,
this is why we thrive to survive
when we are facing what we think is
D e a t h.

There is no such thing as death
as it is a transformation
from mortality to immortality
and a transition from earth to Heaven.

In His era, Christ did not fight
against the inevitable episode
of His life script that He was born for
because He knew He would move
forward and skyward into Heaven
as an immortal into the eternal.

Since His ascension,
He has been our spiritual universal hero.
He is the sovereignty of our inner strength,
safeguarding our spirit that knows of life eternal.

At every given danger, we fight to survive
rather than give up the spirit
because we not yet learned to remember
we will never die.
When the body lays, the spirit rises,
and this is resurrection of immortality,
the reality of the gift of life.

Our spiritual universal hero is always with us
and it is He we look upon at the other end
of the holy rays of light.
He is always there to greet and welcome
our return home from dreadful dream worlds.

This is what it means
to finally spiritually awaken and escape alarming dreams.

Worlds within a World

We spend a lifetime trying to figure out
what the universe is all about.
Great minds who study it
come up with theories of what it is
because they have not yet learned
to remember how to see it
through spiritual vision and knowledge.

Through spiritual vision,
they will know it in all clarity and certainty,
what the universe truly is.
The universe is not a rock, moon or a star,
it is a galaxy and everything we behold in it
are worlds within a world.

Earth is a world and it suspends itself
in the world of the universe
that houses all the other worlds
and everything else in it.

Heaven is a not a place, it is a Kingdom,
but it is the one true galaxy
we will never find
in the vastness of the universe.
We can never reach it
through illusional travels and studies
as long as we keep the world of mind
trapped in illusion, we cannot see beyond it.

Minds of blindness can never enter Heaven
until their willingness to perceive it
through the perception of the Holy Spirit.
This is spiritual awakening into forgiveness.

Of course, everyone has a choice
as to what road they take to spiritually awake.

Worlds within a world is what we behold
and know through physical sight
because the universe is a galaxy too
where we witness all the other worlds in it
as far as our eyes, probes and telescopes can see
along with everything else we propped in it.
Through the eyes of God,
we can behold through spiritual vision,
beyond illusion where we see
the holy, wholly, wholesome Kingdom.

Do you get it?

A Glimpse of Heaven

Everything we see in dreams,
physically perceive and believe brings grief.

In dreams,
love betrays, light turns dark, life dies,
truth deceits, joy is harsh, peace is short,
unity shatters, freedom spirals
and safety is hammered.

Microscopic annoyances bring about illnesses
and weakens the immune system.
There is an atomic universe at war within.
Viruses are at war with bacteria and vice versa.
Dust clings, pollen springs,
hair tangles, skin wrinkles.

In dreams,
in order to stay clean and healthy,
we clean out the colon, take showers,
wash and brush the hair.
Yet no matter how immaculate we believe we are,
atomic war is an all-day, every day emasculation.
We bind each other to the dollar
to pay for stuff we need or want
because on earth
nothing is free, so we say.

In Heaven love prevails, light never dims,
life is infinite, truth sustains, joy is kindness,
peace is restful, unity thrives, freedom blossoms,
safety blooms and royalty expands.
Viruses are friendly, bacteria welcoming,
dust approachable, pollen sociable.

No such thing as digestion, excretion
because everything in Heaven is life
so nothing is consumed or devoured
and not one strand of hair out of place,
and skin is fresh and forever
young and vibrant because you are light.
We never have to shop for anything
because everything is freely given.
God ensures no one is deprived of anything.
This is just a glimpse of what Heaven is.

When we come to learn to behold
and know through spiritual vision and knowledge,
we too will see that everything on earth
is the total opposite of what Heaven is
and this is where we emerge out of denial
and admit to the glory of
God's majestic miracles and our own.

All this and more, is the evidence
of the opposite of what Heaven is.

The Sea of Heaven

Heaven's sea particles sparkle finer than earth's diamonds.

There are almond shape diamonds
that are the clue to every time we cry
through earthly blues.
Yet we are always free to choose,
and can dance in the spirit of bliss,
loving what we do.

The sea of Heaven is
as clear as crystal and as flowy as satin.
There are no waves or ripples
to interrupt its peace.

We can dive deep in Heaven's seas
while we breathe into the abyss of its bliss.
This holy body of water is in such stillness
that there are no currents
to swish you away from the safety of Heaven.

There are no fears to bring about any tears.
Drowning is non-existent and shivering is no reality,
for the molecule spheres of Heaven's sparkly waters
is velvety, warm and comfy.

Not even a speck of darkness exists
in the sea of Heaven,
for its glistening is bright,
full of the vibrance of infinite life.

The deeper we dive into the sparkly sea,
the clearer it becomes, greeting every life form
in passing in this glorious sea of Heaven.

Heaven's body of water is lively and dazzling,

brilliant soulful colors beam aglow,
such a glorious show.

In joy and peace, we interweave
in a dance of light.
Every droplet of the sea of Heaven
greets you sweetly in love, joy and peace;
hovering, swirling, twirling, sliding
and gliding in the exquisiteness of life.

Here, we are filled with glee
under the veil of immortality
where we behold the light in you
and never again will we want to flee.

Heaven, never misleads
and there is Jesus smiling ablaze all happy to see,
once again, we are free to spree joyfully
through the vastness of the sea of Heaven.

Here, we are all too pleased
we returned to our immortality rejoicing in
stillness, love, joy and peace
under the safety of God's cover forever.

The sea of Heaven is certainly a blessing.
It is the upmost holy body of water in paradise,
so serene and free in eternity
where we honor the enjoyment
of its lovely enchantment and our own.

Heaven's sea particles sparkle finer than earth's diamonds.

Mind's Eye

To behold the vastness of the universe
is to traverse into the mind's eye.

Commonly known as the third eye,
through meditation,
a whole new world opens up so wide,
the eye can see it in all its glory.

There is nothing gory, dreary, eerie or boring
about the Kingdom beyond the darkness
of the universe.

It is a world of diverse beautification
under the veil of love and light
with an open sunlit that glistens golden,
where diamonds suspend
in its skies of Heaven.
Seasons do not exist
and treason forbidden.
There is nothing hidden,
for everything is wide open.

Mind quickens to being smitten
to everything already written.
To venture further, the pot celestially thickens
without feeling like a chicken.
He handles us as tender as a kitten
because His elation of love for His creation
is the foundation in which He built His Kingdom.

Under His laws of freedom,
we are free to miscreate
while He peacefully and patiently awaits for time
to enter your date with miracle.

Anyone can be cynical,
but it is truth's empirical.
In other words, it is an experience on a biblical scale
to ensure every individuals mission
to eternal does not fail.
Events are whimsical and mystical
with spiritual vision.
This is where optical illusion is lifted
and where one learns their meaningful mission.

The mind's eye is the sovereignty
of love and light one divinely takes on,
cognitively and consciously
in the spirit of absolute consistency.

There is no decision to make,
for one simply takes the ball and runs with it.

Secrets and Spies

Heaven, a Kingdom of openness
where there is never anything to hide.

There is no such thing
as secrets and spies.
In the making of dream worlds,
we implemented secrets and spies.
This is why we make safes, vaults, bolts and locks
to ensure we block anyone from entering
if they do not have a secret code, key or pass to enter.
We build houses and buildings
with doors, windows and locks
yet every cover up is truly no secret.

We cannot hide ourselves
from an all-seeing and all-knowing God
who brings to light all things done in darkness.
We design to keep others out
or forcefully confine.
We all spy on others, either to be nosey
or stealthy to attack
whomever we wish to devour.
We limit communication
from one end of the world to the other
because we do not exercise
faith and trust in one another.
Then we wonder why we are divided,
when we ourselves close down being united.
Then we walk around wondering why we frown
when our interaction with one another is limited
because we are fearful, paranoid and jealous
or is it something even more sinister?

Fear divides us;
paranoia makes us overthink
believing others have secrets and are spies.
Jealousy dictates ruthless behavior.
Why? Because we have
secrets and spies already built inside.
This is certainly a great lie
as we roam the dream of self-deceit.
To demonstrate a negative attitude
against the figures in dreams
is because it is a reflection
of the darkness within reflecting back at you
and we do not like it
even though it is a stepping stone
to help us find our own way
out of the maze of blindness
and self-deception of secret, spies and lies.

To abolish judgment and merciless thoughts
makes room for forgiveness, humbleness,
kindness, patience and peace to enter,
enabling acceptance, mercy, safety, unity
and freedom to purify and cleanse
our own secrets and spies
inside our own mind.
To reacquaint with mercy and grace
is to squeeze out judgment, persecution
and imprisonment recognizing we ourselves apply the play
of secrets and spies from our own life script.

When we close and lock everything up,
complexity enters
shattering the openness of everything,
making us blind to the reality of freedom.
This is where everything becomes
puzzles and riddles that attempt to solve mysteries.

It has been this way throughout history
trying to find all the pieces to put it all together again.

Heaven's open sunlit from mind-to-mind,
microscopic life forms, to a blade of grass
abolishes the need or desire for secrets and spies.

Heaven's openness is a quantum leap to simplicity
under the veil of love, light, life and truth as one.
By replicating the open sphere of Heaven
and placing everything we made in it by closing it up
brought it to a boil like a pressure cooker.
There came the time
it could no longer uphold
the heat of destruction
and exploded into godzillion pieces.

All the pieces fell where they lay,
including all the dark arts of secrets and spies.

The Decider

God is your Provider, Christ is your Savior
and the Holy Spirit is your Decider.

They are the Trinity
and through their divine qualities,
they work in unison to ensure
our minds' wellness in all of holy righteousness.
It is better to be willing to remember
all of the divine loveliness from your senders
rather than all the earthly ugliness from the ego.

It is a blessing to be willing to let them guide you
through their frequency to the golden road of Heaven,
which is your true dominion.
At one point or another, we pray for the beatification
of sanctification and they hear our pleas
to ensure we receive our miracle.

As the Holy Spirit leads,
let Him be your Decider of every choice
you want to make
because under God's glorious cover,
He is the Decider that never steers you wrong.
Father and brother, always knows best.
They provide the directive to the Holy Spirit,
working in unison to ensure you are at rest
with every decision the Holy Spirit
makes for you and through you.

Consume yourself with your provider,
converse with your Savior
and immerse yourself to your decider.

In them are your treasures
of all your holy pleasures.
As they admire you from above,
they behold your adorability in love.
As they listen to you speak,
they hear the cuteness of your meekness
and as they look upon your behavior,
they see the innocence within.

They look past all the fear and darkness
you embellish onto yourself and others'
and do not hear the nonsense of horrid words
you have spoken or the horrid deeds
as a token to the ego's dictation.
They know all that matters is
the delightfulness that oozes from the core of spirit.
No matter what you think you have done,
God has already forgiven you
because He salvaged you
before you were even born.
This is what enables His eyes
to forever behold the holiness in you.

You are the *chef-d'oeuvre* of His creation
where the spirit returns to the Heavenly Louvre.
It is the galaxy of your solace
where He houses all the loveliness
of your charming creations
as a reminder of the beautification in you.
The Decider is the Holy Spirit
who treasures the *chef-d'oeuvre* of God's creation
without any kind of hesitation
and this goes for all the Sonship.

God is your Provider, Christ is your Savior
and the Holy Spirit is your Decider.

White Dove, Pure Love

It feels we are alone
because it seems we are far from home.

Be of good cheer in all we think, say and do,
for blessings shower upon the crown
of your head to the soles of your feet.
God opens the windows of Heaven,
pours His glistening golden dew
to help us get past whatever comes through.

We are adorable delights in worlds of fright,
be the light, shine ever so bright,
outshine darkness of night
instilled in corruptive minds and our own.

We are temporarily displaced,
born to find our place.
In seclusion on worlds of optical illusion
to find our way to divinity.

Everywhere we go God is with us,
in faith, we know He never leaves us.
With faith, dreams of pains and sorrows fade away
and we know we are never alone.

In stillness, listen to His soft voice
where His Holy Spirit abides
as He awaits we embrace God's grace.
It is majestic to ascend to Heaven
like a white dove with pure love.

Do not be discouraged,
in light, we own courage.

It is okay to make righteous choices,
uphold dignity under the veil of divinity.
God awaits in patience and in peace
to honor our calling.
At the end of the road,
we behold God's golden rainbow aglow.
Remembrance is what outshines
deprivation of our own making.

White dove, pure love is the divinity within.

Upon His Bended Knee

Meditation, is a glorious dedication
to the wonders of humanity's spirit
in all universal and dimensional nations.

Assign yourself a mantra
and let your mind's eye chant it
all the way to the golden altar
where you lay down all the dreadful feats
at God's golden feet.
When I agreed to learn to meditate in all its glory,
the Holy Spirit asked me to pick a mantra.
I gave a puzzled expression and in my mind's eye,
I asked, "What is a mantra?"
He explains that a mantra simply means
a word to focus on through the journey
of the sovereignty of prayer.

The first word that comes to the mind's eye is Heaven,
therefore, I pick Heaven as my mantra.
The Holy Spirit guides me
into the preparation of meditation.
In a space of quietness, I sit on my bed
and bring myself to a comfortable posture.
I close my eyes and bring my mind
to a state of calmness as I focus on Heaven
just as the Holy Spirit said to do.
Then, something phenomenal
begins to happen.

As I find myself voyaging
through the universe inside
making my way to the center of mind,
my spirit joins alongside of me.

We slowly and simultaneously
turn our heads until our eyes meet
in love, joy and peace, *she* smiles at me.

I return the smile,
she stretches out her hand to mine.
I reach back, palms clasp and fingers interlace.
As our fingers interweave in unison,
we smile ablaze.
As I turn my head to gaze ahead,
I telepathically said,
"It's me, my identical twin within has joined in."
We suddenly reach the threshold of Heaven
where we behold a sphere of a golden light
and as we near it, it becomes an open sunlit
where we are witness to the wonders of Heaven.

A glory of angels fly over
the openness of a white sky shimmering golden,
people sweetly smiling ablaze greeting in passing.
In a holy instant, my spirit is at God's golden feet
as He sits on His golden throne.
As I am seated at His feet,
I lay my cheek upon His bended knee.

In pure majestic silence, we sit there enjoying
the unification and connection to one another.
A word, we do not utter,
we simply melt like butter
in the presence of each other.
We join in the unalloyed of love, light, life and truth.
Instinctively, I know
it is only a matter of time I return home.
Never again will I elect to be born
as an experiencer to know what it is like
to be blue under the dreadful skies of dreams.

Separation is fully abolished
the moment I return to Heaven.

Through the voyage to return to the dream,
the spirit of calmness, stillness and peace follows me.
For weeks, I feel I am on cloud nine,
walking on midair
as I now know in certainty,
I am just passing through a bittersweet world
that enters its end.
It is utterly majestic to witness the connection
of the Holiness to the core of His tender and divine heart
under the shroud of love, light, life and truth
which is my own as one.

Through meditation, I find myself at God's golden throne where I sit at His golden feet and lay my cheek upon His bended knee.

Remembering Life Script

Actors congregate to rehearse their movie script
and they might take a wild trip to master the grip of their script.

They summon each other
for successful remembrance of their movie script.
This is a perfect example,
a setup of how to remember
how our own life script came to be born.
No need to sit at a table
waiting for other actors to show up
to study and memorize our own life script.

In the peacefulness of our own home,
all we need to do is call upon the Holy Spirit
who always waits in quietness and stillness
for our willingness to activate our own eagerness
to remember how our life script came to be.
He cultivates our request
when He commits Himself to our enthusiasm
of the holy spasm of our readiness
in the tender ripple that will restore
the part of the mind that is crippled.
This leads to the restoration of remembrance.

The crucifixion is an icon
of affection and tranquility that we fail to behold.
This is why we hate
under the veil of fear and darkness
bringing us to the brink of madness.
The transformation is the example to show
we can go from ruthlessness to righteousness.

The resurrection is the display
of how we can rise from the dead
into redemption to be born again in spirit
where we can alter our life script.

The ascension demonstrates
that Christ returned back home to Heaven.
This is where the Holy Spirit was released
to you and me as we wander through
the duration of time on this world.
His goal is to bless healing
and correction to corrupt thinking.

He is at mind's reach
because the power to summon Him
has always been within
through prayer or meditation.
No one can ever control thought or take power
to gather God's holiest flowers.
His angel wings tenderly tower over
for the safety of minds sanity.

Christ tells us that all we need to do is
be willing to ask and we shall receive.
When we ask for the remembrance
of how we came to write our own life script,
He will be all too pleased
to unveil the answer to our question.
Be steady but ready
for the remembrance of it.
He will not falter at what we ask for
because He plays no idle games
and neither does God.

No need to fear, for the Holy Spirit is here.
It is better to be in a mindful state of seriousness
because what He helps us to remember
is deep, but important stuff.
Through willingness,
all it takes is an invitation
to have a holy conversation with the Holy Spirit.
He is our comforter, guide and teacher.
His ultimate duties are to blanket us
with his comfort through every discomfort,
worry, irritation, awkwardness and anxiety
that attempts to enter
only to spoil your eagerness to righteousness.
These are merely negative forces
that want nothing more than to hinder
what the sender launches
through the Holy Spirit's guidance and teachings.

Through all His comfort,
He guides us to the golden road of Heaven
and shows us what is fabricated and what is factual.
We will be impressed with His willingness
to ease the stress of our life script
and we will be blessed when we remember
how our life script came into existence.

This is where we remember the true purpose behind the acts of the crucifixion, transformation, resurrection and ascension.

Authentic Love

We wish upon a shooting star
hoping to no longer be barred from the love we fearlessly charred.

We believe that when we wish upon a star,
wishes do come true and it will.
It is always best to be mindful
of what we wish upon
and what we wish for.

The astrology of shooting stars are false idols
that mislead, decline, blow up,
blink out and return to stardust.
We witness this
through our brilliant scientific minds who study them.
Sometimes, stars can lead to divinity
like the star that led the three wisemen
to Christ's abode.
It was the ultimate star of astrology
that He made in agreement with the three wisemen
and every soul in existence
before anyone was even born.

This episode of the play
they were born to display
was on a biblical scale.
Even to this day,
it is a divine memorable moment
we read in the Holy Bible.
Look upon the stars
and admire the curiosity of them,
for they are the very elements we made
to temporarily gaze upon
as we try to figure out
how they came about.

Then, refocus your thoughts
and summon the Holy Spirit
to help you remember
we are the makers of every star in the universe
and its galactic communities and dimensions.
Willingness to return to authentic love
is to come out of denial and lay your wishes
upon the golden feet of God's altar
who grants you all the lovely things you ask for.
To wish upon a star might throw you a curveball,
but to bring righteous wishes to Christ,
He ensures they do not waver and fall
because He is the ultimate authentic superstar.

Come out of denial
and rise as Christ's disciples,
for this is the ultimate survival to your divine revival.
Here, we are released
from the imprisonment of thoughts
of denial, homicidal and suicidal behaviors
freeing ourselves from such dreadful chambers.
Recycle such manners to replenish them
and return to authentic love
we have forgotten godzillions ago.
This abolishes all the elements
of the dreary fearsome circle,
freeing you from the bondages of self-deception
where we learn to remember
how to cherish and value
the glistening golden circle of authentic love,
light, life and truth inside.

To release from the bondages
of self-deceit and self-destruction
means to relish and embellish
the glistening golden circle of divinity
within the glorious light of authentic love
you are absolutely worthy of.

Authentic love is the rightful bridal
that does not hurdle you deeper down a spiral.

No Needs in Heaven

I was up all night
so the day became a burden I bore in tiredness.

The insomnia was difficult last night
and though it was a sunny and warm day,
I was cold, bloated and extremely fatigued.
I did not permit myself to sleep
until once again twilight, slowly seeped.
As dawn veils the light,
I close my eyes.
In the morning when I woke,
the tiredness of insomnia
replenished its cloak.

I spoke to God and said,
"O Father in Heaven,
thank you for the restful sleep
all through the night."

In this moment, through spiritual vision,
He permits I behold to remember
there are no needs in Heaven,
not even the need to sleep.
Only in dreams we sleep,
weep, creep, drink, eat, excrete
because this is how it is as a mortal—
a forbidden kingdom that hurts us
because we made everything
turn against us.

When we realized there are no needs in Heaven,
we became spoiled brats and reached out
to grab for a slice of specialness
that God was not willing to fulfill.

He knew by asking to be treated
different from one another
would only bring division to union
and He was not about to grant
that His love be divided.

So we spiraled out of control
and into a kingdom of fear and darkness
where there are needs,
including the need to sleep.

In a kingdom of shattered dreams
and broken promises, union is divided.
Our own love and light
separates from the love and light of God.
He is in us and we in Him
to ensure we are not lost forever.

There is no need to sleep
because we are the vibrance of energies
that vibe for all eternity as immortals.

There will always be needs in dreams,
but there are no needs in Heaven.

I Am Not Trapped

Freedom has always been with me.

Blindness has always been lifted.
The chains and shackles of bondage
have always been loosened.
The door has always been wide open.
The choice to walk through its threshold
has always been mine.
My spirit has always been righteous.
The courage to lay down ruthlessness
has always been in me.

Uncertainty and carelessness
is not of me.
The sovereignty to be alert in all certainty
has always been in me.

Drama is all an act,
calmness is who I am.
Confidence leads to take back independence.
I adopt contentment and leave behind confusion
because I value calmness and stillness
and toss the seeds of thorns.
I forgive God, myself and the Sonship,
this is the key I always held within me,
because I am the key.

The power to overcome the path of boulders
has always been with me,
for it has always been my choice
to choose the path of pebbles
to avoid the road of boulders.

The choice has always been mine to take
the golden road of velvet
to overcome the path of lumpiness.

It has always been in my control
to lay down the frown of an attitude
and accept my holy crown
in kindness, humbleness, patience, peace and gratitude.

I have never been forgotten or abandoned
because the first clone of spirit is always in Heaven.
My worthiness to accept the holy journey
has always been in me.

God is love, light, life and truth.
Therefore, we are all worthy of Him.
I promise,
you will never be bored or blue.

The fun under the veil of eternity
is a reaction to satisfaction.
Never again, will we lose sight
under His delightful love and light.

The feeling of being trapped is temporal,
for there has always been open doors
to free ourselves from the spears of bondage
from the ego's sinister prison.

I stood in misery standing,
screaming for help.
He stretched out His hand
and tenderly pulled me out of the trap.

I returned to rejoice in my worthiness
in His embracement.

He is so enchanting, full of mercy and grace
when I called upon His name,
during a time I believed I never would.

He pulled me out of the pit of fear and darkness
where I emerged under His sparkling love and light
of humbleness and kindness.
This is where I was witness to my divine spirit
at Heaven's gate gazing upon His lovely face.
His eyes compassionately gleam aglow
and instinctively, I know, He is my abode.

Upon my recognition that He is Jesus Christ,
I become a witness to His majestic
glistening golden smile ablaze.
I am ever so grateful that He pulled me out
of such a merciless maze full of devilish haze.
In His glorious presence,
I recognize I am not trapped and never have been.
Nothing is ever what it seems on dream worlds
because it is all self-deceit
that we can holy, wholly defeat.

Freedom has always been with me.

I'm Not Dead

Am I really dead? You say I am! Yet you also say,
"I will see her again because she is in Heaven."

Deep in mind and heart,
we know that Heaven is our eternal home.
Earth is a kingdom of exile
where we experience temporary life.
We know this for certain
because we are witnesses to death on a daily basis.

It is not common to be witnesses to eternal life,
but we are entering this era swiftly
so it will be common to one day be
witnesses to eternal life simultaneously.

To perceive death as real and true
is only a speck of illusional knowledge
until we are willing to escape it
by being willing enough to abolish
puny mentality to grandeur reflecting.

When one learns to behold the big picture
through spiritual vision and knowledge,
everything in this world
becomes meaningless and senseless.
The only thing meaningful and sensible
is the testament to the truth of eternal life.

When you come to refer to death
as a transformation, resurrection and transition,
you will no longer speak of me
as if I were dead because you will know
in all certainty that death is
the greatest act of sorrow and loss.

We have forgotten that we are natural born actors
playing out what we have prewritten.
We also have forgotten the thorns of danger
we anchored at every corner of the world
to ensure there is no safety everywhere we go.
This is why God goes with us everywhere we go.
He upholds His promise to us
that He will not intervene
with our prewritten life script.
He did it for Jesus and He will do it for us.
We hear His soft voice leading us
to the path of safety
or to the exodus from danger
where He lifts pains we endure
through dreadful experiences.

When the time arrives to transform
from mortality to immortality,
resurrect, transition and ascend to Heaven—
we give the greatest performance of
devastating experiences of
the pains and sorrows of loss.

So when the time enters to rise,
I'm not dead and neither are you.
For in the Kingdom of Heaven,
we are more alive than all those left behind
to finish their mission on worlds of illusion.

Since I am in Heaven, how can I be dead?

House of God

Slip into illusion and we find darkness
where we face the dream of conflict against ourselves.

This is where we battle,
trying to find what is real and what is true
only to find madness and blues.
Yet, the clues of peace are not hidden,
It is a world certainly permitted.

For a time, the memory of God is forgotten,
yet it is the house of God we inevitably seek.
In you, His word is written
because by you He is smitten.

When weariness enters—
all worn and tired of battling
against ourselves and the figures in our dreams,
we seek peace
because we want nothing more
for war to cease.

Weariness permits readiness
into the prevalence of peace.
This is the best and swift way holiness enters
lighting up the golden road of Heaven
where we inexorably find the house of God.

The memory of God shines upon
peaceful minds where thanksgiving enters,
grateful for the love and light
we have always known.

Battles, wars and gores are illusions
that bring about holy movements where we recall
that we come from the house of God,
the only golden, vibrant, peaceful
Kingdom of true freedom.

To hurdle ourselves into darkness
is certainly madness.
But when the time arrives when we are released
from fears and sadness and into redemption,
which brings about the remembrance
of who we truly are.

For a time, we toy with what we have never known,
finding our way through the crazed maze
where holy clues lovingly gaze upon
the crown of our heads.
They are always in plain sight,
never hidden, for they are already given.
We can behold this through
the shining light of the house of God.
This is inevitable.

We are scheduled to return
to the only Kingdom we have ever known.

Glistening Waters

On Earth, the oceans and seas sparkle like crystal,
but in Heaven, they glisten brighter than diamonds.

The puny speck of particle sparkle
we see through physical eyes
blinds us to the remembrance
of glistening waters beyond the universe's globe.
Glistening waters in Heaven gleam aglow,
even brighter than the brightest stars in the universe
and the twinkling stars in the earth's night sky.

A sparkle beyond anything
our puny split mind can ever imagine
but we can be witnesses to it
when we behold it through spiritual vision.
Even then, there are no words
to describe Heaven's glistening waters,
for only in the mind's eye can we fathom
the reality of this divine chasm.
As a witness to this glorious scene,
our enthusiasm is so great,
we do our best to describe
the exquisiteness of glistening waters
through earthly words in the hopes of defining it.

Glistening waters in Heaven are alive and well,
full of love, peace and joy
that we delightfully keep in memory.
When we indefinitely return to Heaven,
we forever enjoy being God's golden children.

When we witness glistening waters,
we cheerfully giggle at its holy, loving,
joyful, peaceful and playful nature.

This is a reminder of the holy wholesomeness
of who we truly are.

Part 3
Circle Of Light

The unification of love, light, life and truth
is the fundamental foundation
of everyone and everything belonging to God and Heaven.

Why Me?

We cry out, "Why me?" when things go wrong
as we do not have the grip to be strong.

We wonder what went amiss
when a crime gets dismissed.
Jaw drops at a fake crime scene found
but with evidence of a crime.
Yet, it is false evidence
because it is an act we were born to perform.

We want answers to the violation against us
only because we do not recall
what will befall us at the agreed time appointed.

To remember what has been prewritten
by our very own idea to experience the unthinkable
activates the peaceful agreement between all the Sonship.

It is best to collect the blessings we do not yet see
to behold that we are free.
This is when we will not cry out, "Why me?"

Blessings enable eyes to perceive beyond optical illusion
where we spree under the veil of truth.
Here, it is inevitable to behold that
all cruelty is certainly false.

It is better to have knowledge
to see the decision of our own involvement
in what seems like inescapable deeds
we inflict on one another.

Sometimes, there is no going back to the unavoidable
even when it is not going to be enjoyable.
But we can be at peace with it
if we are willing to see the fake in it.

Remember this:
when the unpreventable becomes a trespass,
it is a miracle that will place us on the path
of moving forward swiftly
when we remember how it brings us
a step closer to God Almighty.

Forgiveness is what brings us out of
soaking in the "Why me?"
Indeed, this is where we find true peace.

We scream out, "Why me?" in desperate plea
to understand why this happened to me.

Broken Wing, Dried Out Stream

The spirit is broken, eyes swollen,
spirit drops to the ground; so weak, droopy and loopy.

Like a bird with a broken wing
circling around on the ground
flapping its healthy wing
hoping to get off the ground.

Eyes swollen because of all the tears flowing.
Through all dreadful experiences, eyes cry
and in moments of more sadness, eyes dry.
like a dried out stream
once teamed with gushing waters,
where life flourished, happy to be nourished.

We can make a strong comeback
even as hearts harden and eyes dry
because under the rays of love and light,
chaotic fire ceases and peace increases.

Through forgiveness,
let the water of tears flood dried out eyes
to wash away the bitter tart of the heart
and let the love and peace in you
awaken to an overflow aglow.

In the light of love and peace,
God enters the realm of dreams
and heals the broken wing.
Bird sings, flies from ground
to hymns of Heaven's angelic sounds.

Empathy of stream replenishes,
red water flows through the refreshing veins
of the heart filled with tears.
Let it pour and rise in holiness,
boldness, wholeness and wholesomeness.

Broken wing, dried out stream,
spirit renewed, tears refilled, birds chirp,
vocals happily sing and tears joyfully flow.

Learn and remember broken wing,
the dried out stream is not forever
if we choose to take a quantum leap
into the realm of love and light
where joy and peace is spiritually uplifting
and where we shorten our sufferings and heal.

It is possible to obtain it in the physical realm
because it is always with you
if you elect to remember it is your inheritance
which you can gain through spiritual vision.

Broken wing, dried out stream
is the act of hope and faith.
Make a tribute to them.
The Son of God heals and restores everything
through honoring His blessings
and your own along with hope and faith.

Broken wing, dried out stream
is the outcome of everything we combat.

Love, Light, Life and Truth

There is a word greater than words we utilize,
a word that describes God in all His glory and divinity all in one.

I asked for this word to be unveiled to me,
for deep in my mind and heart,
I knew there had to be a word
that could describe His combined magnificence.

That word is Grandeur, which includes four words;
love, light, life and truth all in One as follows:

Love = God
Light = Christ
Life = Holy Spirit
Truth = Spirit

What a glorious discovery that is worthy of delivery,
for it is the remembrance of who you are.
A quantum leap forward and heavenward
out of time and into the holy Kingdom of timelessness
where you behold the Grandeur of God
equaling love, light, life and truth in all there is.

Love, light, life and truth = God's divine Grandeur of unity all in one.

This is the essence of the Kingdom of Heaven
you are very familiar with but for a time displaced it,
then renewed and restored remembering you are not alone
in the Grandeur of His love, light, life and truth as follows:

Not alone = One with God
One with God = Not alone

Love, light, life and truth equals
the Grandeur of God's divine wonder
of forever in union.
To remember this
will quench a magnitude of curiosity
as He is the knowledge of who you are,
where you come from and where you will return,
because the Kingdom of Heaven
is your eternal home since godzillions ago.

We are in the era of God
tenderly approaching our realm
from the four corners of the world
to mercifully and gracefully bring your thought pattern
to divine emergent on a grandeur scale.

Be ready and willing to enable suffering from all over the world
and your own to come gently, but swiftly to its end.

Prison within a Prison

The mind is imprisoned, the soul is imprisoned
and the body also is imprisoned.

The mind is imprisoned
in the ego's sinister prison of insanity
because this is what we wanted to experience.
The soul is imprisoned in the body
and the body is imprisoned on a world of dreams
where we are as deaf as an octopi
and as blind as a star nosed mule.

We are all born this way
and this is why we spend a life time
worshipping a loveless and merciless god
that is so puny we do not even notice it.
But we have our senses to help us
hear the peaceful voice of the Holy Spirit
and learn to behold the divinity within.

We first hear the voice of the ego loud and clear
and follow its insane, senseless,
meaningless and backward loudness
because its mouth is bigger than its puny self.

We think backward spiraling downward
writing senseless and meaningless laws
trying to bring insanity of every imprisoned mind to order,
but the world falls deeper into the pit of disorder.

Because when we blame, shame, persecute,
judge, shackle, degrade and cage,
we spiral deeper into the pit
of fear and darkness.

We are a witness to this.
Just look at the prison industry where there is no order
because caging is just as savage as shackling,
judging, persecuting, convicting and imprisoning
which puts us all in a prison within a prison.

For every soul we shackle and cage,
we bondage ourselves to them
because we cannot be free
if we do not permit others
to be free through forgiveness.

Abraham Lincoln once said,
"Those who deny freedom to others,
deserves it not for themselves
and under a just God, cannot long retain it."
To free ourselves from our own savagery,
we must be willing to forgive
the brutality of others and our own.

We must be willing to surrender it
to God's golden feet and let Him heal
and correct the imprisoned minds of insanity.
Always be willing to keep in mind
that the puny god thrives on the insanity
of blame, shame, guilt, shackling, degrading, judging,
convicting and imprisoning each other
in what we call, the victim or perpetrator.

When we bring guilt upon one another—
blame, shame, degrade, shackle, judge, convict and cage,
we become the perpetrator
and this is where we chain ourselves to each other.

We are all in a prison within a prison
as long as we continue to listen to the loud voice of the puny god.

Blasphemy

Blasphemy is not denying
and turning against God and His Holy Spirit.

The mind is sick as it is split,
but it is in the mind
where we are fully healed
to see the triumph of blasphemy.

We think we know what blasphemy means
yet to know what it truly means
is to behold and know it
through the perspective of the Holy Spirit.

No longer are we willing to allow the ego
to steal our birthrights
to behold its malicious blockage
in remembrance of its violations.

The ego demands
the denial of healthy thinking because it flourishes
when we dwell in the foolishness
of its devious demise it leads us to.

Thank God, the Holy Spirit
awaits in patience and in peace
for you to be willing
to no longer blasphemy against yourself.

Only in sickness we worship
and keep false gods we made,
not remembering
why they are a facade that surely fades.

This is blasphemy, not against God,
but against ourselves because the true meaning
of blasphemy is self-annihilation, not God-obliteration.
But we can restore the memory loss
under the cover of God's protection of His Holy Spirit
who enters at our readiness to know the true God.

Be willing to be mindfully healed
and learn to create in holy constructive ways
as God willed us to initiate
and our lovely creations will be fruitful
in all its glorious ways
because it is a representation of God
and He always supports devout ways
for His wealth of knowledge is truly priceless.
It brings us into the brightness of His holy light.

Here, we blossom in His flawless bosom
in all His glorious sweetness
for He is delighted every time
we have chosen wellness of mind
in all its divinity.
Let your light outshine
the ego's perspective of blasphemy
and look at it through the eyes of the Holy Spirit
and you will clearly behold the vicious cycle
where you continuously turn against yourself.

When we praise and worship other gods before Him,
we remain in the vicious cycle of self-deceit
and self-annihilation and this is blasphemy
because the fake gods' we keep
cannot hear our screams for deliverance out
of the fearsome circle inside
that offers torment, grief and death.

It is a vicious cycle revolving around hostility
and denying ourselves and our brothers'
of the truth of God as we continue to listen
to the voice of the ego
or the false and wrathful father we made
so listening and seeing through its perspective
keeps us blind, deaf, and imprisoned.
This is the ancient backbiting sequence
of guilt, shame, judgment, fear,
darkness, pain, and sorrow.

Blasphemy has everything to do
with our willingness to behold the truth of it
through the eyes of the Holy Spirit
who awaits in patience and in peace
to teach us that blasphemy is not against God or Him,
but against ourselves and the whole Sonship.

False blasphemy keeps us blind and in denial
of God's majestic wonders.

Born in the Land of Earth

We are given pills in an attempt to control the behaviors
that insane mental sicknesses dictate.

We are born to be happy in the land of Earth
until episodes enter at its appointed time
to experience dreadful feats.

I was born to experience short-lived happiness
until the time entered to spiral
into the abyss of depression,
anxiety, panic attacks, bipolar
and post-traumatic stress disorder;
labels we put upon each other to give a name
to the mental and emotional issues we wrestle.

Medications are but a temporary fix
that inevitably causes more in-depth symptoms
of adverse reactions to the matter at hand
that we so desperately wish to escape.
We believe what we are told and taught
through the ego's thought network.
These are just other experiences
we are here to encounter.

We are born in the land of earth
as experiencers to encounter bittersweet combats
in its battlefield of dreams
which are merely lessons to learn by.
Living on a world of negative forces
are nonexistent in Heaven,
only positive energy exists
in the Kingdom of Heaven.

Negative energy is not permitted in Heaven
this is why illusional worlds were made
by our own making to be born into
so we can be given the opportunity
to experience what we are not.

Christ tells us we receive what we ask
and we asked to be born into worlds we made
where we can experience fear and darkness.
However, in order for God to approve it,
every soul had to be in agreement.

The moment we are born from out of timelessness
into time, the memory of this is wiped out.
This is why we ask the fundamental questions of blindness;
why, what, where, when, how and are we alone.

Yet, we ask the very minds
that do not know the answer.
Pills do not deliver us
from the mental state of mind
where we spiral into its circle of gloom,
yet we are not forever doomed.
It seems we are eternally lost
even though we can be found.
Our state of mind can be restored
to the vibrancy of who we truly are.

Through forgiveness is where
I once again found my happiness.
I learned to forgive
every individual and life episode I believed
was the cause to my spiraling out of control
and into the depths of insanity.

Through forgiveness, the mind's wellness prevails
and kindness, humbleness,
patience and peace always follows
for they are the fruits of the Holy Spirit—
love, light, life and truth.
This is where insanity is restored to sanity
and is the essence of who we truly are.

At our willingness to forgive everyone and everything,
we permit God to bless His divine miracles
upon the crown of our head
lifting us from the dead.

This is where I was delivered
from all the medications
that were prescribed to me as a temporary method
to tweak my thinking to control behavior
for it is how we think and what we believe
that will dictate how we behave.

Born in the land of earth,
we are here to learn and remember
how to forgive one another
through every dreadful episode
we encounter as experiencers.

Through willingness to forgive,
we overcome the insanity of mental illness
of every appalling experience
on the battlefield of hideous.

This is where we are divinely lifted
into the realm of love, light, life and truth,
washing away all blues.

When we are born into the land of earth,
we seek righteous celestial forces
while we are lost hoping to be found.
Rest assured, at its appointed time,
your miracle to deliverance and redemption
from insanity is bound to enter.

Restoration to the mind's wellness prevails
under the veil of love's absolute sovereignty.

It Is Not Easy

It is heartbreaking to live in a dream of illusions
filled with loss, chaos, tragedy, trauma and destruction.

Compassion and comfort is needed
in a world full of dreadful deeds seeded.
The battles, wars and gores are defensive and senseless
which leaves us breathless in weary weakness.

It is not easy
hearing screams of pains and sorrows,
then to be asked to rejoice in it
and utilize peace and compassion
in your passion to forgive and console.

To remember it is
an illusion of events we asked to experience
brings the fear of it to a calmness.

It is not easy
facing evil and wicked encounters
but to remember we agreed to it
does bring a chuckle.

It is not easy
but the forgiveness and remembrance of it
is where we gain the tranquility
and innocence of it in every encounter
we do to ourselves and one another.

It is not easy but through forgiveness,
we are released and redeemed.

In this holy instant, we behold and know
in certitude the innocence
of the act of all evil endeavors.

The effects of feeling the illusions
is what makes it seem so real when really it is surreal.

A Wolf Disguised

A wolf disguised as a sheep, sly and sheik
as clever as a golden retriever.

A hunter eyeballing whom to devour
but, how much longer
will one choose to be
a wolf in sheep's clothing?

The wolf goes where the senses of its nose leads,
for the insidious hunger overpowers the desire
to acquire qualities of a sheep.

As a wolf disguised in sheep's clothing,
one is charming, but ever so ruling,
for the gentle and charming ways masks
one's ruthless and aggressive slays.

Blind to what is right from wrong,
but deep inside desires to acquire
peaceful ways of a sheep and tries to be discreet.

One feeds their wolf tactics and is out of control
and one takes off the kind disguise
when you are blocked with nowhere else to go.

Illuminate your sheep ways
and let the wolf in you croak.
Do not sigh over what is right,
lay down the wolf's cloak
and give love and peace a loving stroke.

A wolf disguised is a wolf in sheep's clothing,
a deceitful cloak that can give you a stroke.

Be willing then, to lift the wolf within
and rise alongside of Christ
who loves you with all His might.

Feed the sheep and you will rise,
feed the wolf and you howl for love and relief.

The Pranks We Play

The pranks we play are the acts
of the glistening golden diamond super stars we truly are.

In this dream world, there is a seriousness
in all of the pranks we play
that we become furious and ferocious
with one another.

Time and time again, we fail to realize
that everything we experience
are the pre-written pranks
we agreed to play one to another.

The pranks we play are the roles
of your own show and my own
and that makes us *all*
glistening golden diamond super star actors.

The seriousness of this is of vital importance
to learn and remember
that the pranks we roleplay are an act.

We enable ourselves to remove
the seriousness, meaninglessness and senselessness
of the roles we play.

We permit ourselves to move forward
into the realm of the loveliness
of whom we truly are.

We are mind and spirit, the cleanliness of
love, light, life, and truth;
the truth which is in you and all the Sonship
is pure holiness.

If we had been willing to behold this at the crucifixion,
we would had embraced Christ
in love, joy, peace and forgiveness.

We would have shook his hand
congratulating Him for such a great act
of suffering and death
and we certainly would have remembered
that we asked Him to prove His love for us
by pretending there is such a thing
as suffering, mortality and death
but this does not mean we need to do the same
to prove our love for one another.
It would be plain foolishness because Christ does not ask
that we prove our love for Him or each other.
Christ knows that deep down inside
that we love one another, God and Heaven.
Denying it is no issue
because the day enters when we remember.

Christ was taken down from the cross long ago
and He asks that we refocus our attention
to the transformation, resurrection and ascension.

This helps us release each other from
guilt, shame, blame, judgment,
conviction, punishment, and imprisonment.
This is where we are willing
to free Christ from His own sufferings
from the cross and the crown of thorns.

To release Christ from the crown of thorns
is to honor Him with the crown of white lilies.
It is a quantum leap into peace
where we become witnesses
to the miraculous release from His sufferings.

We witness His transformation
from bloody to beauty, injured to healed
and frail to sovereignty.

To honor Him with the crown of white lilies
is to restore Him to the glistening golden champion
He truly is and where we embrace the gift of immortality
under the glory of eternal beauty.

This is how we free ourselves and the Sonship
from our own life script of sufferings.
All it takes is a willingness
to learn and remember
not to take this dream world so seriously—
the realm in which
we condemn one to another.

At willingness to forgive,
we behold past flesh and bones
which is a quantum leap into the lovely reflection
of who we all truly are.

We become witnesses to the holiness inside
and we giggle at all the pranks we play
because in all certainty, we see clearly
how boring, meaningless and senseless it truly is.

We will no longer have an interest
to roleplay any and all mercilessness
because egoistical thinking will be abolished
and miracle thinking will arise
to flourish in all of its magnificent glory.

The beautification within attracts the adornment in others
and we want nothing more than to share it forward.

We excitedly urge others to be willing
to see the loveliness in themselves
to behold it in everyone and everything else.
It becomes a reflection of the naturalness
and sameness in all life's purpose.
This permits us to lighten up on the pranks we play
like a domino effect enabling the light within
to light up brighter than the fiery sun
in the universe's atmosphere.

In dream worlds, forgiveness is always key
to enable us to let go of the dreams
that inevitably go into oblivion.
This shows off the beautification
of the true essence inside in all its glory
where we are spiritually equal to Him.
This is not arrogance,
it is His chef d'oeuvre of cloning.

It is better to let God shine His love and light
upon us and through us.

It is Up to You to Choose

To escape any frightful situation
is to choose wisely who you scream out to.

When falling into a bottomless crevasse,
you desperately struggle to grasp onto its sidewalls
only to slip from your own grip
through this ghastly trip.

Through its horrid situations,
you scream to be released into the bosom of His love
when you find yourself in beastly circumstances.

Under a divine thicket of hugs and kisses
are treasures of fortunes;
loyalty to your heavenly royalty
and it is up to you to choose Heaven or hell.

I hope you choose
divinely, wisely, carefully and precisely
because God is an Almighty Father
who gives us free will and will not pluck you
out of the heat of dreadful illusions
if you choose to stay there.

Only the true God can hear you
yet it is up to you to choose who you scream out to.

Self-Awareness

Looking back at the chaotic kingdom you stepped out of becomes meaningless.

Walk out of the dream
look back and see how you stepped out
of a world so chaotic and blurry
but you are not worried.

To step out of the dream
is to step into true reality
where you are suddenly fully aware
of whom you truly are
for you now see past it
to a Kingdom of love, joy and peace
where you are a witness
and where you instinctively know you are home
and this is God's grace.

You stretch out your hand as if to touch it,
for you realize it is parallel to the world
you just stepped out off.
You recognize it is so close,
yet ever so far.
You notice you cannot enter it
because it is not yet your time.

You step back into the dream fully self-aware
of whom you are and where you come from
because you intuitively know
the meaningful Kingdom is your home.

The only self-awareness that is significant
is the love, joy and peace
that adoringly consumes you
for in that holy instant,
you are in true self-awareness
where you feel excitedly self-contained
and self-confident of oneself
because of your own recognition
of the Kingdom from which you belong.

Would you like to know how to wake from the dream?

Holy Ministry

Ministry,
a holy industry of who we truly are.

There is an appointed moment
in a world of time
when the miracle we are entitled to
finds us.

A holy frontier where we do not tear
for there is no fear in a holy instant
of the occurrence of a miracle.
In a holy instant, we transform
from who or what we think we are
to whom we truly are.

Such a holy discovery
enlightens our mind and spirit to full recovery
through the encounter of God's miracles.
Here we will seek, find and study
the holy event we wish to buddy
and at our appointed time,
the answers to our miracle surely enters.
The truth is, we reunite
in the realism of God and Heaven.

We are pleasantly surprised
at our appointed demise,
that the holy ministry is already inside.

Holy ministry is a golden gift
implanted inside at creation
and we are born with it;
knowledge for a time forgotten
but will surely emerge from our remembrance
and we confidently embrace it in faith.

Holy ministry is a poetic clergy
of the glistening circle of hope.

Shh of Silence

Through the duration of time on dream worlds, the shh of silence can be achieved through chaotic relationships and global changes.

Sometimes, silence is the best form of communication.
One day, without hesitation,
I bowed to this dictation.

I found that this is true in the days of fears and blues.
Although, it is a challenge to hold the tongue
and slip into the realm of silence
to uphold kindness, humbleness, patience, peace and faith
but it still can be done.

The blessing to the shh of silence
is stillness and calmness
even through all the ferocity and anxiety,
silence is ever so calming.

To go against the shh of silence,
only causes mental and emotional imbalance
where we crumble
in the middle of senseless mumble jumble.

Every day, all day, we worship to speak out in a heartbeat
without any consideration of the thoughts we blurt out
so we fall deeper into self-deceit and self-destruction.
Then we wonder why we spiral down the chaotic pit
of fear and darkness wondering what just happened.

When we hear the soft peaceful voice of Christ
say in the midst of dilemma,

"Shh, close your eyes, bow your head
and remain in a moment of silence.
This will pass, do not ignite
the heat of gas with a match,
for she is my child."

Through the turmoil of a friendship,
faith enters, lo and behold,
I hear and listen to the exact words of Christ.

As I close my eyes and bow my head,
the babbling of an angered voice fades into the background.
His words just about took my breath away,
yet I breathe a sigh of relief
that my heart is no longer speared.

My own anger is lifted
from feeling I wanted to bash and smash,
and scream out to shut up
so she would stop saying hurtful things
and behaving so radically.

In moments of anger or hurt,
we all can get ferocious and treacherous
in the choice of words
that come out of our mouth.

Because I complied to Christ,
He grants a holy moment and lifts my spirit
into the peace of His light
where I watch her jabbering on all by herself
as I watch from above in peace and silence.

Then, while peace befalls me,
sleep fell upon her and she slept through
the whole five hour drive from there to home.

I remain in the shh of silence
and the despair of anxiety and sorrow
were no longer dwelling in my mind and heart
and my tummy remained still.
This brought my mind and heart back to balance
where joy prevailed.

I am grateful that through my willingness to listen,
Christ honored my obedience
and plucked me from the sadness of her words
and the anxiety of her behavior.
This brought nothing more
but bliss and peace the whole way home
through my silence.

This lesson was at a time
I was determined to learn of spirituality.
This event was my chance
to hear, listen and obey His instruction.
I am grateful to my willingness to honor his words,
for I was victorious to this experience
by remaining in the shh of silence.

As I drive all the way home in silence,
my already fractured spirit was shattered.
I thought, *"How can I be in peace*
and feel the shatter of my soul?"

When I walk through the door of my home,
the essence of sadness consumes me.
I fall to my knees and plea to restore my soul
for there are no words to describe what it is like
to feel the soul shatter into godzillion pieces.
It is an experience beyond words.
You would have to experience it yourself
to know what it is like.

Christ enters my realm
and cloaks me with a cape of royalty
and rewards me
with the restoration of my crushed spirit.
As I mindfully forgive her,
happiness consumes me from head to toe.
He never spoke, but I instinctively knew
He restored my soul in the shh of silence.

Through forgiveness and restoration of spirit,
it cleansed away all anxiety and sadness,
restoring joy to the core of my soul.
I was at total peace with everything I had endured on that day
and to this day, peace and happiness prevails.

This experience was another stepping stone
on the journey to learning spirituality.
I persevere in His teachings and this is why
I can now write about spirituality on a deeper level.

When we are obedient to the calling of holiness,
our spiritual education can only flourish
under the guidance of God's Holy Spirit.

To learn and understand spirituality on a deeper level
takes courage and willingness to permit holiness to enter.
These are holy instances where Christ arrives in our realm,
permitting us to hear and listen
to His soft peaceful Voice, particularly,
whilst in the midst of turmoil.

This is where we have the chance to remember
to be calm in the midst of a storm
where we experience
the stillness of the shh of silence.

This is where we are witnesses
to the holiness and sinlessness
in the renovation of
mind, body, soul and relationships.

This is a blessing on a grandeur scale,
enabling the situation to go into oblivion
permitting the relationship to remain intact.
What a wondrous spiritual event
to experience and witness!

Because of His divine intervention,
my friend and I are able to maintain
our friendship in peace.
I am appreciative of this
because sometimes, we all have a bad day.

Through silence, we can get through any situation
in peace with people we know,
people we do not know and have not yet met
because we are all the same
in ruthless games we play.

We are born into dream worlds we made
to have the chance for such experiences
that are not permitted in Heaven
and through forgiveness,
we can see this clearly where we prevail
under the veil of love and light.

The shh of silence is of vital importance
in order to uphold relationships in love and peace.

I See the False of Insanity

Through the eyes of deception, we have witnessed
all the foolish and twisted ideas of misconception.

There is nothing on this world worth valuing more
than mothers, fathers, brothers, sisters and all the others.
O child of light, we can shine so bright
as we abolish the act of frights and flights.

We are all brilliant actors
and this is simply a dream world factor
as we roam upside down and backward
as earth's axis remains tilted.

Just when we think
we have seen it all or heard it all,
another twist of self-deceit
falls at the base of our feet.

Through every blight we all combat,
we can behold the act of every crazy, messy
and testy ideas into oblivion where we gain true freedom.

I see the false of insanity,
come and behold it with me.
Let's elbow together and value each other.
Through forgiveness, we can do this.

This enables us to move from backward to forward
in the loveliness of joy and peace
because you see, you too will see
the false of insanity at willingness
to let God lift the veil of vanity.

Forgiveness permits the lift of blitz.
This is where we behold the holiness
and sinlessness in you
and me giving a sigh of relief,
letting go of all the grief.

For to see the false of insanity
is to behold the truth of sanity
which is the main factor within you and me
and this is what forgiveness brings.

I see the false of insanity
because I elect to forgive, forget and move upright
and forward in the holiness of love, joy and peace.
On dream worlds, they are the most pleasant spirit of gifts
to enable ourselves to shift
from a horizontal axis of madness
to a vertical axis of wellness.
This is where we no longer freefall
down the shaft of a cliff.

The blue, green, brown and white planet
we call Earth is a stage where we traverse.

Deep Thought

Did it all start with stardust
or did stardust start with imagination?

I say creation begins
with minds of inventiveness.

Who are the minds?
Well, I say, we are the minds.

Okay, who created the minds?
Well, I say, God created the spirit
with genius minds.

Then who created God?
I say, God is self-created.

What about colorful creations?
Colorful creations are derived from Heaven—
the colors there are nothing
like the colors in galactic dimensional dreams.

The moment colors are manifested into dream worlds,
their euphoria becomes expelled.
This is where they are not as vibrant as they are in Heaven
because they lose the glory of their essence.
This goes for everyone and everything else
born into dream worlds.

Yet despite it being lost for a time,
it can be found and restored
to its natural state of vibrancy.

As we witness the brightness of a lighthouse lantern,
we wonder what happened to its colors of illumination.
We seek it in the constellation craft,
not remembering colors creation
is in the altar of minds' holy cognition.

We can behold it if we are willing to meditate on it
and when we do, the euphoria expelled is restored.

This is where we can clearly see
the glistening colorful creations of Heaven,
brings pure elation through remembrance
to the genius mind we are all born with.

Only for a time, we have amnesia
until we are willing to reverse it
through prayer or meditation
which unveils recognition to everything
one wants to know and behold
in the deepest thoughts of holy cognition.

Euphoria expelled transforms to ecstasy essence
where we behold the vibrance of Heaven's colorful creations
that tenderly outshines any and all clusters
of constellation craft of every star in the universe.

While we are blind with amnesia,
we believe stardust made us
when truly, we made it and this is the twist.

So I ask you this,
how can stars be our creator
when it does not have a mind to design?

We are the ones with the mind
so it would make sense
that we are the ones who designed
all things seen in the constellation craft
and everywhere else in the universe
and in dimensional cosmoses.

*Where do you think stardust
as well as everything else started from?*

Sex Most Sinless

The sin of sex comes from the ego's thoughts,
which is the guideline humanities' insanity.

God created Eve for Adam in the Garden of Eden
and told them to multiply on the Earth and be fruitful.
Therefore sex is not a sin
and if it is seen as such, it is being interpreted
from the doctrine of the ego.

God ordained and sanctified sex
as part of the temporal life on Earth.
This has nothing to do with the ego
telling us that Eve sinned
by eating the forbidden fruit from the tree
of knowledge containing good and evil.
God would not do this to us.
He would not put a tree
of knowledge containing good and evil
in the Garden of Eden and then tell us
that we were forbidden to eat from it
because this is where
temptation comes into play.

This would be plain maliciousness
and there is no malice in God.
He is a God of love and righteousness.
We are acting out in mercilessness
through the ego's perception
because of the strange presence of temptation.

O Child of God,
there is a bubble of pure senselessness
to make each other feel guilt and worthlessness
under the umbrella of sinfulness.

It is better to embrace the intimacy of sex
that God blessed for it is not sinful
but it is an opportunity to be born into
the worlds of illusion to experience what we are not.

This is the effectiveness of what has already been
prewritten before we were even born.
It is a sick excitement to experience
the opposite of what love and light is.
When we learn the lessons of fear and darkness,
we remember that all good and positive forces
come from God
and all bad and negative forces
come from the ego,
also known as the devil, enemy, serpent
and many more names it has been given.

To know precisely right from wrong
is to be spiritually awake to make better choices.
This gives us the chance to embrace righteousness,
which abolishes any and all wrongfulness.
It is a merciless act to force sex upon another
because making someone do what they do not want to do
is not of God but comes from our own doctrine
through the ego's twisted perspective.

Guilt and shame is not of God
because they are negative forces
that blame each other for their choices
to make sick decisions that bring upon cruel afflictions.

When we admit without pride
that we are the children of God
who made a merciless god,
we begin the journey of feeling guiltless and worthy
of the one and only righteous God
through His tender cleansing and purification
of the ego's ruthless thinking.

We learn to respect what another does not want.
It is also a learned encounter to respect
the agreement of sex most sinless to one another
where it is a beautiful occurrence in all its goodness.
It is dazzling to know sex most sinless
in all its righteousness—
which is a reality of pleasant ecstasy
to be in accord in harmony's symphony
of this trance state of pleasure
for it abolishes the temptation
of inviting forcefulness into it.

To respectfully be in agreement,
abolishes forcefulness, guiltiness, shame
and feelings of unworthiness and sex becomes
the glorious symphony of ecstasy it should be
where the parties are pleasantly pleased.

Sex most sinless is enjoyable
through mutual respect of each other.

Trapped

In certainty, I behold holiness,
yet I elect sinfulness.

I feel so trapped, yet I see the gap.
From afar, I am now at an open door
yet I turn to walk towards
the threshold of a closed door.

I remember the righteous one
yet I choose the ruthless one.
I feel the holy calmness,
yet I dramatize most thoughtless.

I behold the freedom of confidence,
yet I fall deep into gloominess.
I feel the holy contentment,
yet I hang onto restlessness.

I'm in the midst of stillness and quietness,
yet like wild wind in a storm,
I whirl around
planting seeds of thorns.

He leads me to the path of pebbles,
yet I take the path of boulders.
He hands me my holy crown,
yet all I do is pass it up with a frown.

As long as I refuse to heed to His calling,
I spiral deeper into the circle of gloom,
this is simply a pity party of doom.

After recognizing these blessings and refusing them,
I have the nerve to ask
when my blessings will be released
from being trapped in the ego's sinister prison.

He leads me to the golden path of velvetiness,
yet I step onto the road of roughness
and I feel trapped
because I elected to remain blind and deaf
to His gifts already given.
I prefer to keep brawling with myself.

I remember I must forgive, yet I protest.

Light in the Mist of Shadows

The light in the mist of shadows is Christ
who lifts your spirit.

He's in the mist of every shadow
where you might be battered or bothered,
but it is He who plucks the spirit
to the safety of His bosom.

In those moments you feel no pain,
He lifts you up in His strength
and in that holy instant, you gain composure
where you let His peace be your enclosure.
You remember the light in the mist of shadows
is He who is within and who loves you
and will not forsake you.

Through His lead, you learn to follow Him
from out of the dreadful shadows
and into a world so different and anew.
You knew this glorious world before
and you are confident it is your natural home.

In those moments, you watch the battlefield from above
and you remember He who raises the spirit
loves you beyond enough.

You painlessly know He safeguards your sanity
as your spirit watches such senseless tragedies.
This is where you are grateful you can be redeemed
because it's all but just a dream.

Receive the peace given to you
when you are in the center of a battlefield
because the light in the mist of shadows is Christ
who lifts the spirit from all hellish bulldoze
where one can certainly come to the brink of discompose.

Receive the peace given to you
when you are in the center of a battlefield.

My Story is Yours and Your Story Is Mine

My story is yours and your story is mine.

We do not remember that everything we experience
falls under the agreement.
We are acting out every miscreation we made.

Before we were born,
we wrote our deepest, darkest thoughts
that would be events we would experience
to the end of time in agreement with each other.
We wrote we would speak
of our most unthinkable experiences
of sufferings, squealing on one another.

When I snitch on you, I am squealing on myself
and when you snitch on me, you are squealing on yourself.
The agreement works both ways.

At the end of time, none of it will even matter
because when we return
to the holiness of love and light,
it supersedes all fear and darkness
we had encountered.

In the presence of God's love,
nothing else matters
and this is the core of His divine miracles.
We will not even remember
what we went through anyway
because the memory of it
will all be dissolved
along with the end of time.

This is the miracle
of the sovereignty of His love and light,
even more so experienced when combined.

In other words, all the ancient crimes
done to one another is obliterated
because it is meaningless and senseless stuff.
When we reenter Heaven,
we return to the holiness of immortality.
Here, we walk upon golden streets
smiling and greeting each other
with eternal love, joy and peace
that will never cease.
This is a holy atmosphere,
so pure and clean where there is
never anything to fear or tear about.

This Kingdom is so lovely and vast,
it is a holy bay of beautiful creations
you and I get to share forever
where there are many wonderful things to explore
that boredom is non-existent.
Creation is never ending.
This is the true reality of a Kingdom untainted
where we awaited godzillions to return to.

Are you ready to willingly be reacquainted
with whom you truly are
and where you come from?

At our readiness, we break the chains and shackles
of bondage to tattle on each other to the end of time
because at remembrance of the agreement,
we giggle at all the acts we were born to experience.

The agreement we entered into before time began
makes my story yours and your story mine
no matter the beauty or how gory the story is.

Positive and negative forces clash in a world of time,
and crime does persist through distorted harmful events
that we insist on worshipping.

Everything that happens
in each and every lifetime
is what we signed up for.

To be disgusted with what another has done,
is to be sickened with yourself.
The only reason we find dreadful feats
so shocking is because of our own memory loss
of what we agreed to.

It does not matter if one thinks to commit
a horrid deed or acts on it,
because thinking it and doing it are the same thing.
In other words, when we think it,
we are just as sick as the one who does it.

To remember that my story is yours
and your story is mine is to admit and accept
that all stories are connected.

Whether we are a party to it or not,
the connection is there through the agreement.

When we admit that
the reality of horrid experiences are fake,
we lessen its power to keep us
in its chains and shackles of pains and sorrows
because beastly experiences are not real;
though it is the giving into temptation
at the root of all evil
that makes for rotten humans.

His light outshines all ruthless misfortunes
on worlds of gloominess within my story and your own.

Perfection vs. Imperfection

Heaven is perfect and earth is imperfect
so how does one define perfection vs. imperfection?

What if I told you that we are
co-creators with God in the creation of Heaven
and the making of Earth, the universe and everything in it?
What if I told you that we are
co-authors of our own life scripts that we wrote in Heaven
of what we would encounter on Earth
before we were even born there to live out
our brilliant yet destructive episodes?

Would you believe it? At first, probably not,
but this is where
perfection vs. imperfection comes in,
for God is perfect.

Since He is our creator, this makes us faultless
because He created us flawless
but for the speck of darkness
that began in the heart of Lucifer.
God asked him to let go of this
before it fully manifested itself.
However, he did not pay any heed
to this advice of wisdom because here we are
on a world of imperfection
because we agreed to follow God's beautiful fallen angel
which makes us fallen saints
who fall short of God's glory.

When we permit the Holy Spirit
to teach and guide us to the golden road of Heaven,
we elect the simplex way of learning and remembering
because with Him, nothing is complex.

It becomes a divine trip
because to look through the eyes of God
is to behold the essence of perfection vs. imperfection
and to see how it is equal to simplicity,
for He removes complexity
from His teachings with guidance.

When we are able to see the ease of it
is only when we recognize how
He had gently hurdled us through quantum leap—
the journey where we learn and remember
that there is no need to weep
and even if you do,
He is there to comfort you.

When we do weep, it is merely from tears of joy
while remembering that all the devastation was just a ploy.
We might feel some guilt or shame,
but there is no need to worry,
for God's Holy Spirit nips it in the bud
with His royal cloak of comfort.

This is what removing complexity does
for it enables us to see clearly
that there is no shame or guilt
in the imperfection of our own makings
of self-deception and self-destruction
because God permitted us to miscreate
and does not condemn us
for making worlds He authorized.

Since everything on Earth
is the total opposite of Heaven,
we easily forget this on a world
that is too busy following dreams.

However, we are now in the era
to remember it through willingness
because we can still follow our dreams
as we hope to be redeemed.

My brief defining moment of redemption came
when I was willing to behold it
through the eyes of the Holy Spirit
for this is where clarity and certainty entered
under the veil of simplicity
to honor everyone and everything
no matter its form.

When fear is brought upon us,
we remember to bless love upon it.

When darkness befalls us,
we remember the light within and the glory of God and
Heaven.

When one values or devalues mortality viewed outward,
we remember to value the holiness of immortality inside.

When one threatens to kill us,
we remember we are life eternal.

When one tries to imprison us,
we remember we are freedom.

When separation is thrust upon us,
we remember union.

When the ego tries to hurdle us into sadness,
we remember we are happiness.

When meandering minds bring conflict upon us,
we remember the peace within.

When it hurdles us into danger,
we remember the safety of God.

When it tries to throttle us into guiltiness
we remember our innocence.

When it tries to pass judgment upon us,
we remember God loves and accepts us as we are.

We remember the imperfections of the loveless force we made
where the essence of perfection lays.

We behold the love and light of celestial ways God created,
which is flawless and makes everyone and everything within
perfect.

Perfection vs. imperfection helps us to remember
the perfection of God's chef d' oeuvre.

Change or Chaos

Have you ever seen and heard fear
in the expressions and voices of everyone
who tells their story of traumatization?

They share their story in sincerity
because their pain and sorrow is very real,
for they have not yet learned
nor do they remember that the effects of their experiences
are nothing more but a dream
that can seem very real and natural.

Only in worlds of illusion does the reality of dreams
full of fears, tears and troubles exist
and where we will feel the effects
of the pains and sorrows of fear and loss.
The ambiance of such experiences
is why we believe it is real.

The reality of it is so dramatic it is pathetic.
At our willingness to observe it through this perspective
is an open door to learn how to perceive it through spiritual vision.

After we get through it, we find ourselves yawning
because it gets very boring as a witness
to the dramatization of dreams,
day after day and night after night
and day after day and night after night.

When we finally see the dream and remember,
it is all but an act of fake events that are so ancient,
we cannot even remember how old we truly are.

By the time we reach this point, we will be so ready
to return home to Heaven where we will recall
that there are no dreams to try and wake from
as we take in the purity of Heaven's fresh and clean aroma.
Heaven is so pure and clean,
there is never any mess to clean up
and life there is so impeccable
that despicable things are not permitted.

Safety is a lifetime guarantee in the true sense of the term
because God does not permit phases of modifications.
For revolution is chaos
and calmness is harmonious,
the symphony of creation
where peacefulness reigns
and this is why we are forever joyful
under the cover of God's love, light and safety
where we lavish in our royalties.

Chaos is unnatural,
whereas calmness is natural,
the essence of creation.
It is better to be wary
about taking dreams too seriously.

The only thing we must consider
and take extremely seriously is our eternal future.
This day arrives when our spirits will rise
to transition from the makeshift kingdom
to the genuine Kingdom.

All momentary globes are always revolving,
but Heaven is full of consistency,
sustaining love, light, life and truth forevermore.

When the desire to awake from the dream enters,
we have to face the choice to continue to stay asleep
by taking the fake life seriously
where nothing is ever as it seems
or wake up to fill our bellies with laughter
at the joke that is on us through our own making.
From generation to generation,
this is what we remember to say
in recognition of chaos.
But in Heaven, everything is exactly as it is
for there are no baubles of toys
that wobble to deceive the eye of the beholder
from what is fake or real.

Do we want a kingdom where we grow tired
of all the senseless and meaningless chaos of constant change
or do we want a Kingdom where we can witness
the lovely exquisiteness of creation for all time?

Heaven is where we will never grow weary of anything
because fear, darkness, pains, sorrows,
loss and chaos are nonexistent.

Existing within peace and calmness, it is inevitable
that we will grow very tired of all the drama of the world.

The Choice Is Yours

Each person that we bondage criminal acts to,
we also chain and shackle ourselves for this is how it works.

God's laws of freedom permit us
to miscreate dream worlds and be born into them
where we can make the ultimate choice
we will all inevitably take.

When we rebelled against God,
He did not shackle, punish or imprison us
when we fell short of His glory
and into the temptations of brutalization.

He simply permitted us to miscreate worlds
where we can go and be born
to live what we wanted to become and we did.

We do just the opposite of what God did,
we chain, shackle, judge, convict, punish
and imprison those who fall
into the temptations of brutalization.

The choice is yours
to come out of your own attraction
to wicked decisions that bring about the beast
and to recall the calmness of peace
because you see,
to chain, shackle, judge, convict, punish
and imprison is just as savage.
It is wise to learn to remember this
if we so wish to be free
from our own sick bondages of temptation.

Freedom is inevitable
because the day and hour enters
when we want nothing more than to be free
from the burdens of the ego's sinister prison.
You yourself will be set free
to explore and experience
what you were born for.

Everyone falls into the ego's lure
to control, judge, punish, chain and cage
where we will never be free
until we learn to let others be free
to be who they are here to be
and do what they are here to do.

The choice is yours to be free
from the ego's evil strongholds
by permitting others to be free to be
who they are born to be.

Let God do His miracles of healing and correcting
our insane ideas of thinking, saying and doing
so our own wickedness can be redeemed.

The choice is yours to let others be who they were born to be
and what they were born to experience.

Hounding Justice

It is the spirit of forgiveness that sets us free
from all the pains and sorrows this world offers.

In a world of disorder,
we make up laws to bind the ways
of hateful and spiteful attacks one to another.

We use plastic ties or metal fastens
to restrain the hands that take a bold stand
to bring pain, suffering and death to others.

We seek to cage the evil ways of others
only to find it causes one to slip
deeper into madness.

When one has done their time,
the doors to the iron cage open
to finally let the punished one roam free.

We think they have learned their lesson
and will not yearn to steal, kill and destroy again
only to discover that evil has intensified and become worse.

The disciplined are now free to do
whatever they please and though we think they are at ease
and believe that their lessons have been learned.

There is no justice in chastisement
just as there is no righteousness in hounding justice
for others taken in a brutal fashion.

We think hounding justice for the one gone
from the world of destruction brings peace
and rest to the departed.

The reality is they are at peace,
more than you will ever be during your duration
on a world built on a foundation of destruction.

The departed are now among the living
for they are no longer in this world of brutality
where everyone is walking backward spiraling downward.

The departed are blessed to be
in the safety of our Father in Heaven
knowing hounding justice for them is meaningless.

For they are alive and well among the living
in the enjoyment of a painless free world
where there is no suffering.

It encourages us to move forward
in forgiving and loving ways as a reminder
to not bind each other to the evil ways of others.

To unbind the plastic ties and metal fastens
from the very hands that took the evil stand against another
will free you from the pains of trespass and the sorrows of loss.

Forgiveness is the way
to unbind your own chains and shackles
that bind your own unforgiving ways to the egotistic flays.

Unlock the cages
and forgive their evil phases
to unbind their wicked ways and your own.

The ties that bind drop off to no longer be in bondage.

This is leadership from out of fear and darkness
to the threshold of love and light
into the splendor where eyes behold
the rebirth of their ways and your own.
Willingness to take the flight into forgiveness
means to be a witness through spiritual vision.
This is where one feels a heavy load of pain
and sorrow rise from the mind and heart.

Rejoice in everyone's freedom and your own
from the insanity of fear and darkness
and into the sanity of love and light
obliterating blasphemous to righteousness.
Learn to know that the ones gone
and whom we seek justice for are alive and well
more than we ever will be
on this world where we are left behind
to complete our journey through imprisoned time.

Hounding justice is just your way
of trying to ease your own pain and sorrow,
which are selfish feats.

Electing to bind them to our sickness,
we bind ourselves to our own ways of craziness.

Truth of Life

Seek the clues inside and you will find them.
All it takes is willingness.

I am not delusional of the truth of life
for I have been taken into the depths of holy, miraculous thinking.

The reality is
I am obsessed, elated and consumed
with the truth because it is love and joy
in the eternal ecstasy of holiness and peace.
Anyone can learn to remember to focus on the truth,
which takes away all earthly blues.
Do not let it boggle your mind for too long,
stay strong in the sight of Christ
and you heist in His Almighty light.

Every voice that calls upon His name is heard
and plucked into His bosom
in the cosmos of His sovereignty,
love and light, Heaven's delight.
He lifts you into a painless realm so familiar,
we become aware through the instinct of holiness
that this truly is our home.

Heavenly home is shown where the mind is blown
and we instinctively know as we say in awe,
Here, I stay, never again to play
in a world full of frightful days and nights.
Through your own miracle,
do not be surprised when you are told you will survive
to return to share the reality of Heaven
in the joy of love, light, life and truth.

Upon the return from Heaven to earth,
there is no doubt you defend your testimony to no end.
This permits you to stay in the very sight of love and light
Which is the truth of eternity.
When you have the experience of your own miracle,
there is no doubt you will
forever be thankful in the magnitude of gratitude
to voice the testimonial truth of life.

In the Heavenly realm, there are no illusional dreams.
Heaven teams of true reality in the tender intensity of
everyone's destiny.

There is nothing abnormal about miracles,
they are factual and natural.

Spark the Light in You and Me

The spark permits love, joy, and peace to enter
with blessings of bliss ever so swift.

No longer do I simmer
where light was once dimmer
for I am attracted
to the divinity of His glimmer.

A golden glisten of light shines upon my mind
where I behold that no one
is a sinner, not even a beggar.

His Holy Spirit sparks the light in you and me
and we see the innocence reflecting the way to detecting
that we are the connection to redemption in one another.

Mind to mind, we remember the holy agreement
of senseless bereavement and we smile
at the thought of our amnesia,
for in that holy instant, we remember
the foolishness of that devastating design
of such an agreement between you and I.

Spark the light in you and me
and together we behold
this fear and darkness we made
and now wish to desert it.
It is then that we no longer keep our distance
but come together in a holy blaze of glory.

Palm to palm, our fingers interlace,
softly gripping through mercy and grace.

We lean forehead to forehead,
eye to eye nudging gently closer
as we rise to the remembrance
of the disclosure of the agreement
between you and me.

Spark the light in you and me
and together,
we will see the loveliness
of our holiness and innocence.

Now side by side, we turn eye to eye,
smile to smile, hand in hand,
we walk ever so tenderly upon
the darkness of the land.

Each step we take brightens the way
for the light in us keeps us at bay.
How can it not?
For it lights up underneath our feet
where no one can defeat.

Now in the fullness of His light,
we see the madness of the bittersweet arrangement
between you and me.

To move forward together,
we spark the light in you and me,
which gets us through horrid feats.
We once again dwell in the splendor of exquisiteness
where the holy creativity
of pleasantness, beautifulness and innocence
beholds the loveliness
of love, joy, and peace in all its glory.

Spark the light in you and me,
for together we outshine evil deeds and wicked leads.

No Crime

We label what we perceive
as troubled and evil deeds as a crime.

We give it the name the ego tells us to give it
and neglect to summon the Holy Spirit.
Through prayer comes enlightenment
to be led to the remembrance of forgiveness
where we enable all things to fall
as they are prewritten at every call.

We listen to the ego
and accuse one another of a crime,
the very word the devil loves to hear us say
because when we put the label of crime on the other,
it gets in the way of God doing His part
to bring blessings upon the mess we made.

Do not force yourself upon me,
let me be free to embrace you and me willingly.
When I love you and you love me what
does it matter what age we need to be?

Their ages drastically differ,
let it be the way she wrote her script
to be in agreement with him.
Not only by he and she,
but also with all the Sonship.
We interfere and separate the inevitable
because we do not remember the agreement
made between she, him and everyone
born on a world to experience disagreements.

We are so forgetful
because we label her a criminal
and he becomes the victim
when in true reality there is no crime.

In their mutual love for each other,
they both willingly act upon it lovingly and tenderly.
When we love mutually, willingly
or forcefully and unwillingly;
either way, we label it as a crime.

We observe it this way in time,
but in the Kingdom of Heaven
God knows there is no crime
in what is to take place in its given time.

For what we do to one another,
we agreed to when we were in Heaven
brainstorming our earthly bittersweet hell storms
before we were even born
from timelessness into time.

When the time arrives, we are horrified
at the collision of evil or loving deeds
where in true reality there is no crime in any fashion
of the formation of every good or bad feats.

No crime is what God sees
and as long as we are not willing to behold through His eyes,
we remain blind to the remembrance
that we are the authors of the pre-written life scripts
we all agreed to in everything we think, say and do,
which are merely the experiences
we are here to act out and honor.

How can we ever be free to willingly love
when we elect to perceive it as a crime?

Prisons' Demons

Demons have no qualms
about invading the peacefulness of thoughts.

My mind was consumed
on how to evade and survive hateful creatures
that thrive on vicious features.

Through nightmares of thought,
it was a horrific invasion of monstrous demons
who had no pangs to bang my head
against a stoned cell wall in the pit of hell.

In the equation of ossification,
I look up and plea for sanctification
as I bleed from head to toe
with hanging flesh abrasions.

Their black long pointy tongues
lick their lips and gnash their teeth
as if they just finished a meal
or were about to devour God's little girl.
There is nothing about these hellish realities
that appeal so I finally scream out,
Jesus take the wheel!

The monstrous creatures
are preposterous creepers,
their outrageous schemes
are after one thing only,
to inflict terror upon my soul
to bind me
in burning red flames of control.

Then in a holy instant from a distance,
fresh golden glistening fire enters.
Its warmth is a breeze of selcouth
and its aroma is a miracle of elysian.

Out of the mist of golden fire,
emerges a figure
and as He approaches closer,
I gain composure.

With each step He takes, instinctively I know,
He is an efflorescence anew
like psithurism, a gentle breeze of delight
in this dungeon of fright.

With each gesture He makes,
each thought He gives,
gleams aglow
like a sweet mellifluous to my ears.

These monstrous creatures
are powerless in His presence.
They move aside and bow away
as Christ makes His majestic way
down the corridor to the prison cell
in this pit of hell.

Under the veil of Heavens sovereignty,
I had no scintilla of doubt
that He will release me from the grip
of these torturous prison demons that were
a perturbing, merciless experience.
I know I did not need to beckon
because He knows exactly where I am imprisoned.

Beware, for everyone is holy, wholly, wholesome;
look through the eyes of bold
as we have always been told.
We are not victims, we are victors—
no matter the images of these frightening figures
with their manners in prisons' demons
that scissor in cerebral patterns,
always remember,
that we shine brighter than hell's fire.

He is the Almighty kalon, the amaranthine of an undying flower
in the midst of Armageddon.

Shattered Thoughts

O why do my thoughts bring on such fought?

A battle of mixed emotions,
I want to drop my devotion.

The wrestling match
makes me want to dash,
but I do not wish to struggle
in the throttle of my deepest troubles.

I sometimes feel the goal of it shatters
like a tipped over glass-top table
the forceful wind blew over
and it exploded into millions of pieces.

Is this a sign of the unkind ego
or the feeling of uncertainty
through my journey
to completion in certainty?

I desperately wish to pick up
the fragments of the shattered glass
to piece the bits back together again
to see the meaning of the reasoning
behind my shattered thoughts.

I asked for a sign to tell me
if my shattered thoughts were confined
or if your thoughts and mine are safe to share
when I clearly see many are not ready to care.

O Father, through discernment,
I behold the shattered glass as symbolic
to the vision of my shattered thoughts.

As I watch the battered world divide,
I pray for their willingness to unite.

Through the voyage
of my spiritual education with the Holy Spirit,
you have always told me:
It is only a matter of time
when events of illusion unfold
as they are prewritten.

The time has come where we move
from backward to forward
turning the horizontal axis to a vertical axis
reaching God's throne
where we no longer roam and moan
under the veil of pains and sorrows.
This is the ultimate unfolding
of everything that has been prewritten.

I pick up all the fragments of the shattered glass
and as I sit puzzling over it, I clearly behold
it is the ego that attempts to shatter my peace of mind.
During these times, I am content to share
the deepest thoughts of God and mine.

The ego is a mind game
that always attempts to bring down the hammer
to shatter holiest of thoughts.
It is the destroyer,
the essence of its making
that always seeks to demolish.
I have learned to discern how to disown
its merciless thought patterns
to enable myself to be in God's will.

Stay in the merciful thinking
of God's love, light, faith and miracles.

The Fear of Love

The fear of love is our own distorted perception
because God did not give us what we asked for
when we were still in Heaven.

Fear is propped at every corner of the globe
by our own crazy ideas of what we wrote
to encounter at the time of its arrival.

We will fear it when we run into it
because we have not yet learned to remember
that through grace our fears will be released.
We agreed to every misdeed
we drummed up to experience.
Are you not just a little curious?

When we were ready,
we let the fear of love consume us.
God is not whom we ought to fear
even though He permitted us to experience it.
We asked to be treated special
from a spoiled brat's perspective.
We thought Christ was being treated in a special manner,
failing to recognize that we are all special
in the eyes and heart of God.

This gesture speared His heart
as He witnessed the speck of blackness
at the core of our own heart.

We permitted the speck of darkness
in the heart to manifest
and this is where God knew
we would be separated from Him and Heaven.

It was a moment of devastation
knowing He would honor separation
under His laws of freedom.
However, separation is not His Will
and neither is it truly ours.

God gave us the option to either love or fear
because we cannot have both.
Every single soul had to be in agreement
to the separation process in order for God to approve it.
We all entered into an agreement to make a father
that will give us what we asked for.

Yet, we have forgotten the stipulation
that it would not give us
what we would end up begging for.

We would beg for our life
because we made a loveless father
that is ruthless in offering nothing
but fears, pains, sorrows, tears and bloodshed
and the belief that death is real.

Yet, we do not fear it
for the evidence of it
is all over this merciless world.
The proof of not fearing it is the reality
of homelessness, starvation, pains, sorrows
and the bloodshed we bring upon one to another.

We do not bother to be willing to remember
that it is the ego who dictates behavior
through merciless thoughts.
We do not let God heal
and correct our corrupt thinking
in order to abolish such senseless reasoning.

We worship guilt, judgment, conviction,
punishment and imprisonment.
The evidence of the ego is in plain sight
yet we are blind to it.

We easily accept the loveless father we made
because we believe we are special
and deserve justice of punishment
when we encounter its merciless dangers
at the hands of another.

The true translation of the phrase,
fear God is, fear Love.
He is the One we turn to for protection.
We scream out His name
for His help and safety
when the wickedness of fears
and tears of danger comes a trespassing.
Here, we instinctively know
that God has always been our safety net
in the Kingdom of Heaven,
the home from which we are from.

The fear of love is pointless
because God is the one
who always shines His light
upon the very tears and shivers we are slave to.
He shows us the way out
and into His bubble of safety.

Upon the call of His name,
His light always outshines
the thoughts of the fortress of hard knocks
that want to see us tremble
in fears, tears, pains, sorrows and bloodshed
because He is the only way
to deliverance and redemption.

Even though God approved illusions of such nonsense,
it does not mean He agreed to it.
He simply refused to single any of us out
by granting the special treatment we asked for.
Singling each and every one of us out,
would mean He would have to tear down
the wholly, holy, wholesomeness
of Heaven and the Sonship.
He was not about to do that
and this is why He gave us a choice
between love and fear.

It is obvious we elected to experience
this fabricated kingdom
where we tremble in the fear of love
exploring the vastness of darkness
as experiencers and dreamers.
I am so grateful it is a temporary and crazy fabrication
to one day return to holy, wholly, wholesome adoration.

To find swift release from toils and snares
is to journey to the altar of mind,
a quantum leap where we find God.

Most Delightful

O, how I was mistaken to believe
you abandoned me in a world of spoils, toils and snares.

You have never forsaken me most delightful.

O, how I was mistaken to dare
believe you did not care for me.

You give insightful compassion most delightful.

O, how I was mistaken to agree
to the slayings and pains of this world.

Your mercy is a blessing most delightful.

O, how I was mistaken to agree
to be born into a world full of disgrace.

Your grace remains most delightful.

O, how I was mistaken to reach
such a decision to be born on a loveless world.

Your love prevails most delightful.

O how I was mistaken to settle
on a joyless world that only brings on tears of pains and sorrows.

Your joy triumphs most delightful.

O how I was mistaken to concur
to live on a world of uproars full of battles, wars and gores.

Your peace pours most delightful.

O, how I was mistaken to agree
to experience what it means to tremble in fear.

You are always near to wipe away the tears most delightful.

O, how I was mistaken to believe
I would be able to see in a world of darkness
full of dreadful dreams.

Your light inevitably shines most delightful.

O, how I was mistaken to think
that I would hear your voice in a cluttered and noisy world.

Your calmness in me
remains in the midst of messiness most delightful.

O, how I was mistaken to think
you were reckless in letting me spiral out of control
and onto a world feeling so all alone.

Your devout ways are always with me most delightful.

O, how I was mistaken to look
upon the flesh in sinful and unholy ways of the Sonship.

Your holiness and sinlessness triumphs within me most delightful.

O, how I was mistaken to think
I could see through the misty fog of dusk.

Your lovely light leads me out of the maze of gloom
ever most delightful.

O how I was mistaken to want
to be born into a world of boundaries.

Heaven is a welcoming Kingdom
under the open sunlit most delightful.

I now clearly see the wonderment of Heaven
where there are no doors to lock,
windows to latch and borders to secure,
where nothing is blocked and in complete stillness.

On behalf of all your lovely souls,
I thank you for your hallowed ways.
They are with us through all our days
to lead us safely and peacefully
out of the circumstances of fear and darkness.

Your glorious love and light is where you await
to embrace us to the center of your tender Heart.

I was mistaken, O Father in Heaven, to believe
through godzillion years the violations came from you
when you are ever most delightful.

True Love

O, how sweet is His love,
filled with contentment and sacrament.

We seek love in a bottle
of beer, whisky, rum or wine.
We seek love in needles,
shooting drugs into our veins.
We smoke it, toke it and snort it
consuming ourselves in it time and time again.
We seek it in one another,
not remembering we are love
and loved by the Most High
looking vertically upon us.

He awaits patiently in love and peace
for your prearranged time
to reacquaint in the grandeur of His miracles.
All you need is a fraction of His love potion
to place you in the blissfulness
of a locomotion of His love
that is yours and mine.

Holy love never fades in a world
caving of the love of a bottle of liquor,
the love of needles,
the love to smoke,
the love to toke
and the love to snort.

Discover His holy love
and throw away what you think you love
because the holy love in you and me
never fades while everything
we think we love caves.

As the curtain gently flows down,
the crown of love is unveiled
and will definitely prevail.
This is where you see and hear
as it now shows and tells the truth
of the holy love in you and me
that gently brings you forward
into the light of His devotion and adoration.

All those who have the strong desire
to abandon all corruption and self-destruction
to see the true love you seek,
come unto our Father in Heaven
and He honors you with all of Him
to once again emerge your true love with His.

God is the only true love for you and your true love for Him
and this is how it always has been.

Simultaneous

Fallen saints,
born to paint bittersweet worlds red,
like that old saying:
we leave the house to paint the town red.

Born to play with toys we made
until we are done clowning around.
Leaving Heaven is what causes depression
and all the other ill sensations follow
only to heed to the calling to experience brawling.

Everyone gets their chance to know
what it's like to be and feel
lonely and unloved
the moment we leave our beloved.
On the ground of which you land,
you gaze around to feel alone and banned.
At the unfamiliar surroundings,
the findings are frightening;
an exertion that feels it will last forever.

Dream worlds are illusions
and this ensures, it comes to its conclusion.
This different land of which you stand
seems deserted of other life forms,
spiraling you down into a state
of bleakness and dismal emptiness.

Like that old saying:
it feels like there is a hole in my heart,
I feel like something is missing.
This desolation is deception.

Soon others arrive as you travel through
what seems like a maze of a forbidden world.

Animals soon emerge from the woodwork
and even herds of them soon run upon the land.
As you are a witness to these events,
you are shocked but also content.

You thought you were alone
because you do not recall
you are a fallen saint along with other souls
that soon fill the world.
It does not matter the appearance they arrive in
because all life forms are born out of Heaven
and God loves all of His creation.

The story of the population on earth
began with Adam.
God assisted Adam into a deep sleep to dream.
The day and hour enters
when God awakens Adam to meet Eve
in the Garden of Eden.

Godzillions ago,
separation is zapped into motion
by our own crazy notion
to temporarily leave God and Heaven,
where each soul fallen is never forgotten.

Through separation, one by one,
we are all born into Adam's dream and our own.
Here, we experience phases
of madness, sadness and pleasures.
Episodes prewritten prior to artificial insemination
from Heaven to earth to physically grow
and birth out of a woman's womb.

This is the genesis of synthetic cloning.

Here, we experience condoning
one to another through false love and separation,
not remembering it is the act of self-deception.
As time goes on, we grow tired
of loveless and lonely attitudes
as we seek for love and comfort
in all the wrong places.
This is an act of the phases we all go through
and we do so through selfish and merciless thinking
of the ego's sad and mad dictations.

Time and time again, we fail to achieve
authentic love and union
because we have not learned
to rise from synthetic fear and separation
to learn of the great emergent.

Merciless thinking results in ruthless behavior.
All this brings is tiredness of such merciless temptation
where we scream out for God's redemption.
Time is nearing simultaneous greeting,
like a domino effect
from one side of the world to the next.

Through the love of miracle thinking,
we easily forgive laying all destruction
at God's glistening golden feet
for healing and correction honoring His laws
of forgiveness, atonement and redemption
in preparation for the great emergent.

Time is near to rise out of synthetic fear and darkness
to behold God's glistening golden light
of His simultaneous miracles.

This is where He fills the hole in the heart
as a reminder to us that He is the missing link.

We have reached the era of willingness
to let God do His miracles simultaneous
to once and for all authentically love, forgive and freely bless
the survival of humanity in upmost decency.
This is where we begin to emerge
from Adam's dream and our own,
the grandeur plan of redemption
to the great emergent.

Patience is a virtue
from the depth of the minds' amnesia.

Pure Fulfillment

No longer are there misty valleys
upon this land of happy.

In the misty valleys of shining silver thunder storms,
falls glistening balls of golden snowflakes.

They glide effortlessly
from glistening golden white skies
into a Kingdom waiting to rise.
They take the eyes for a ride
as the mist clears within the valleys' hyde.
As the valley awakes to its demise,
the land begins to rise.

Mountain peaks grow,
the landscape fluently goes with the flow.
Through a water portal,
its flotation welcoming waves
make a grand entrance.
In the midst of creation's water waves,
they carve the valleys' foundation.

This scene is not an aquamarine dream
but the theme of new creation.

Welcoming waves glisten golden
with purple sparkles upon its surface.
A golden moon rises
with specks of glistening purple
upon its horizon.
It's a dazzling new moon of wisdom
in this Kingdom of harmonious rhythm.

Its dynamic charisma
is a reality of enigma
until one beholds the vision
of this Kingdom's true wisdom.
This is a spectacular mindful moment
when one is ready
to come to their divine senses.

It is a potent growth of focus
within spoken words of discernment
that leads to atonement
that is patiently and peacefully awaiting
to bring pure fulfillment
in all its glistening golden brilliance.

No longer are there misty valleys
upon this land of happy.

Holy, Holy, Holy Child of Light

You are the reflection of
He who is within.

Holy, holy, holy child of light
shining ever so bright.
You are holy in all your devout ways,
not recalling this as you dabble
in senseless riddles and plays.
For you are the holy light under His feet
and this is ever so neat,
particularly when you heed
to great deeds.

Holy, holy, holy child of light
shining ever so bright
as you wander under His light,
particularly,
when you accept Christ's atonement.

Here, you are as holy and sinless as can be,
a light aglow under your feet with every step you take
for you are the light of God's love
glistening through the veins
of every brother you save.

Holy, holy, holy child of light,
the essence of God's joy.
Put away all senseless toys
and let your peaceful joy spread
throughout the world and into the universe
for you are as holy and peaceful as can be.
Light shines upon every word you say,
every phrase you convey
and every gesture you display.

Blessings shower upon the crown of your head
to the soles of your feet
as God shines His light
upon you and through you
at your willingness
to receive Christ's atonement.

You are holy, holy, holy, child of light
pure love, full of the essentials of joyfulness,
peacefulness, humbleness and kindness,
the innocence of your essence along with patience.

Holy, holy, holy child of light,
God loves you with all His might.

A Child's Reflection

We enter various phases of experiences
through time.

Babies and children
are not the only ones that are innocent,
for we are all born innocent.

Our innocence does not crumble to dust;
it will be lost through the stages of time,
though it can be found.
Day to day,
we witness our innocence
time and time again,
but we do this blindly.

We behold our innocence
through a child's reflection
which is the epitome of
a man and woman's innocence.
We are blind to this
because we think adults should know
right from wrong.

There is no such thing
as right from wrong
because it is a game of illusion
to reach holiness no matter how old we are.
We are all children
until we are willing to perceive
through spiritual vision and knowledge.

Here is where we see
the big picture of the puny kingdom
full of mischievous miscreations
but we also view the Kingdom
of well-beloved creations.

At our willingness to know the truth
about everyone and everything,
God lifts us out of the pit of darkness
and into the realm of light.
Here is where our perception
is healed and corrected and we gain
the knowledge of both worlds.
This is where we behold and know
in all clarity and certainty that
the kingdom of the universe is a false world
from which we do not belong.

This does not bring sadness,
it brings happiness to learn
that a world full of pains and sorrows
is a kingdom that enters its end.
When we gaze upon the other world,
we blissfully rejoice that the Kingdom of Heaven
is the real world from which we do belong.

This does not bring sorrow,
but fills the mind, heart and spirit
with utter joy to learn that
a world full of love and light
is the Kingdom of timelessness
that never enters its end.

To receive gifts of spiritual vision and knowledge
that has already been given means that
the remembrance of the Kingdom of Heaven
prevails inevitably.

The next time you are face to face
with a baby or child,
allow yourself to be a witness
of your own reflection in them
and them in you,
because a child's reflection
is your innocence.

We will all witness one day
that a child's reflection lies in your innocence.

Sphere of God's Golden Light

No reason to roll the dice to the genesis
of how I came to pay the price.

Feeling tired and worn down,
living in a frown.
I accept the crown
of knowledge and understanding.
Let me flourish in its divine expanding.
I shall dance with them in twirls and swirls,
intertwining in the sphere
of God's golden white vine
of purity and brightness.

As I relax without being tense,
I feel at home in its presence
knowing it is such a blessing.
Through the eyes of holiness, it all makes sense.
Lovingly, I gaze upon vibrant light
outshining all fright, fight and flight.
I embrace its magnificence,
knowing this is what is most significant.
Where there is glum comes enlightenment
on earth's environment.
I am not bummed
nor am I ever shunned.
In the sphere of God's golden light,
wisdom and understanding
are so vivacious and outstanding.
They are swift to tenderly outshine
the intense mood of frights, fights and flights.

Time to end the bloody,
get rid of all the money
we believe is the root of all evil.

Embrace the sphere of God's golden light
with all your might.
The urge to emerge intensifies
godzillion times over.
Join the graceful dance for the chance to emerge
in the sphere of God's golden light
that is as easy as breathing and is so comforting.
Tiredness dissipates into nothingness.
Teetering and tottering uplifts
into a soft rising wind of holy energy.
The sovereignty of God's golden sphere of light
outshines all weariness and eeriness
of frights, fights and flights.

Here, ego thinking goes
abolishing its merciless defiance
for it interrupts God's holy directive
to the restoration of our hearts' desire to be
holy, wholly, wholesome minded
where His love and light sustains it
on a grandeur scale.
His sovereignty uplifts the spirit
where we are completely content
because we clearly behold
we never again deal in contempt.
It is most beautiful to be grateful
to journey through immortality.
Within the sphere of God's golden light,
we love with all our might.
This is what truly matters.
The sphere of God's golden light
is indeed a blessing.
This is not a means of trespassing,
not when happiness and peace gracefully enters
with a dazzling song and dance
owning its divine stance.

The beauty of it is the essence
of its divine influence.
No need to be concerned with interference
for it is non-existent.
When we are at home to no longer roam ancient battlefields,
illusion ceases its annoying intrusion.

The ancient dream is a mirage to cloak the truth
of the sphere of God's golden light
that easily outshines all chimeras through His divine aura.
The circle of light is already inside since time began.

It is possible to behold the sphere of God's golden light within
if we are willing to look.

Threesome of Forever-Some

Father, Son and Holy Spirit
are the threesome of forever-some!

Father, Son and Holy Spirit
are brilliant in guiding us through
every phase of the illusional world we made.

God's stipulation of miracles
implemented in every life script on earth
is the most loving and magnificent idea
that we will forever be
grateful and thankful for.

O Father in Heaven,
thank you for your tender majestic miracles
of love, light, life and truth.

Let Rest Befall Me

My eyes are heavy, yet my mind is wide awake.
Mood is somber as much as a wanderer.

I wish to lay my head to rest,
yet mind is as dreadful as a twisted pretzel.
Let peace befall me, let stillness comfort me.
Be gone insomnia, for I am ready
for the embracement into God's bosom.

Then I slip into meditation to enter God's Kingdom.
I do find complete stillness.
The peace of sentiment into contentment
where I declare holy settlement.

There is nothing more lovely
than to cuddle into the warmth of God's cushion.
Such a comfy bosom where I find rest
under the safety of the softness
in the openness of God's holy nest.

He let rest befall me while I am dreaming
to no longer fall into the weeping of insomnia.
I elect to settle in the peace of His bosom
where I rest and sleep in stillness and peace.

Let me sleep as deep as a sheep.

I Softly Surrender

He embraces me as if I am
a precious diamond He uncontestably treasures.

In the setting of a majestic hospital
feeling not one speck of hostility
not even a frown as I wear a hospice gown.

Wearing ordinary attire,
she lovingly takes my hand where I stand
and leads me through the corridors
of the glorious hospital where I see
there are no doors at every room.

At every turn, there is a party
arising in every room we pass.
I feel puzzled,
yet I do not feel an ounce of gloom.

Glorious soft music plays
as everyone smiles ablaze with a friendly gaze.
I feel utterly amazed
at the angelic hymn of wonder.

The guests are dressed divinely, dancing gracefully.
As I fix my eyes upon their lovely faces,
they greet me with a bow
as they telepathically welcome me.

I instinctively know I am ill,
but I am calm and still.
She tenderly releases my hand
so I may walk among the enjoyable party
as the guests continue to gracefully smile and dance.

As I elegantly glide through the party room,
I gaze upon the lovely vibrance of its decorations
relishing in Heavenly angelic music
I had never since heard.

To my delight, a tender mellow buzz of a golden bee
swirls around me with adoringly ease.
Eye to eye we smile upon each other
and telepathically speaking,
she greets me sweetly with a warm welcome,
then, she exquisitely wings away.

My guide once again tenderly takes my hand
and escorts me out the doorway of the party room
and steers me to an open door
where there is a darkened corridor
I do not wish to enter.

We approach the threshold of the open door
where I stand and bow my head in humbleness and stillness.
With my feet planted, I instinctively know
once I cross the threshold,
I will hear the music no more.

In that humbling moment, my only desire is
to remain at this door's entrance
for listening to such glorious angelic hymns
brings me great contentment.

Not wanting to go up yonder,
my feet remain planted as I ponder.
Then I telepathically tell her,
I do not want to cross the threshold.

Never saying a word,
she gives me a gentle nudge
gesturing me to cross the threshold.

I keep my feet planted and remain still.
Still never saying a word,
she motions with another soothing nudge
to walk past the threshold.

Instinctively, I know she knows I am bold
and that in delight, I would behold
and hold dear to my heart
what is on the other side of
the darkened corridor.

Through my own courage,
I step past the threshold,
she follows behind me
and the door closes gently.
I no longer hear the Heavenly music I so adored,
but I already knew I would not hear
its angelic softness once the door closes.
I bow my head, thinking, "Am I dead?"

In this dimness,
I find myself in magnificent silence
under the veil of total stillness.
I sense the essence of tranquility
and I am immediately aware
of His Majestic presence.

Still with my head bowed,
she gestures me to walk down the dim corridor
and when I do, something marvelous happens.
With each step I take, the way brightens
and when I lift up my head,
I am witness to the beauty of His Majestic
devoutness, completeness and goodness.

His pure white shining bright light
is all around Him where He stands
at the other end of the corridor with a welcoming smile
and wide open arms ready to receive me.

As I continue to walk to Him,
I instinctively know I have always loved Him
and He has always loved me.
Intuitively, I know I will never again
fall away from His love.
I knew that since godzillions ago,
He patiently and peacefully awaited my return home.

She gently delivers me
to thy Majesty and bows away.
As I stand before Him,
I gaze into His loving eyes and want nothing more
than to plunge myself into His wide open arms.
So I softly surrender into His loving arms.
Naturally, I know I will not be harmed.

I fondly clutch my arms around His waist
and I lace my left cheek upon His chest.
He lovingly wraps His arms around me
and gracefully lays His right cheek
upon the crown of my head
just as He had done many times before
in the earthly realm.
In His glorious silence and compassion,
He lets me feel the love and peace of His heart
and I understand where the term,
Heart of gold is derived from.

I softly surrender,
realizing I am no longer sick or dead.
I am alive and well
in the majestic bosom of His adoring heart.

Intuitively, I know He is eternal love,
light, life and truth—
the foundation of holiness, wholeness, wholesomeness,
joyfulness and peacefulness forevermore
in the imperial Kingdom of Heaven
where I am utterly speechless.

His heart does not pulse, flutter or beat.
It is an effortless sphere of flow, a glisten glow of pure gold.

Telepathic

We think we are alone in our thinking.
The truth is we all talk telepathically to each other
and many times instantaneously.

There are instances when we telepathically speak
to one another simultaneously
in face to face conversation
or in distance, we telepathically
think it or speak to each other.

We say things like,
"I was just thinking of that"
or "I was just about to say that"
or "I had the same idea."

We think of it as imitation or being odd,
because the memory of connected minds
have been wiped out from our remembrance
from the moment we are born into time.
Memory loss is the setup we agreed to
in order to experience thoughts of greed
in words, phrases and ideas.

Telepathic thinking exist
on a world shrinking in greed,
for we live on a world of time that will
one day end with a great sigh
returning to our original state of minds shared.

Because telepathic thinking derives
from Heaven and is eternal.
This is part of the essence
of our immortal nature.

The Kingdom of Heaven is where
telepathic thinking originates from,
where there is freedom and sharing,
where we never have to pay a penny,
dime or quarter for telepathic communication.

In the Kingdom of Heaven,
we live easily in this world full of fresh and breezily air.
We live peacefully and effortlessly in telepathic thinking
where we share all thoughts and ideas freely and generously
without being selfish and greedy.

All thoughts come from Heaven
and this is what we must be willing
to recognize and accept, to once and for all,
shut down selfishness and greediness of
words, phrases and ideas that you believe are yours alone.

Telepathic thoughts are not copies or creepy
because this is how we communicate in Heaven.
All thoughts are freely and generously shared
and this is one of God's gifts
we must be willing to receive on worlds of dreams.

My thoughts are yours
and your thoughts are mine.

Connected Minds

Let us behold that my ideas are theirs
and their ideas are mine.

O Father, for too long I felt mindfully disconnected
in a world twirled in tornadoes of confusion.
O let me no longer stew in misperception
of a world in such disorder and disconnection.

Let me behold the Kingdom of Heaven
in all clarity connecting Your Will
with mine and mine with Yours.
Let uncertainty be of holy certainty.

Let me connect with the Sonship and them with me.
Show us the vision of minds linkage
for my aim is to fill with joy
as I finally once again behold our thoughts joined.

Let us relearn this to remember to generously
share everything with all the Sonship
through every relationship and friendship
abolishing foolish ideas of infringement and plagiarism.

Lead us to the recognition
of divine sovereignty to be charitably connected
for our thoughts and ideas combined
is strength most kind and the way to miracle thinking.

Let us behold the holy glistening golden cord
to connected minds
where it leads us to the Kingdom
where we initially and thoughtfully joined.

Let us not bind our ways
in loneliness and greediness
for all it does is bring wretchedness and treachery,
which only leads to negligence and selfishness.

Bless us with the fullness of happiness
in the rediscovery of connected minds.
Here, we see our togetherness
in oneness with you.

O child of light, let's have a parade
in celebration of this holy breakthrough
for it is a memorable holy union
that brings down the veil of separation.

Release the greed
and let our thoughts and ideas
created in loveliness be generously shared and accepted
for this brings power of unification without feeling invaded.

Here, we will not be frightened or fight
because generosity will be our nature
and we will see clearly how we have
always created lovely things together.

We always claim that power is in prayer,
but too often we neglect that power is also in sharing.
This, we have forgotten for a little while,
but it is now time to remember.

To be willing to share everything freely
without cost or trade is the ultimate miracle thinking
that emerges from minds of selfishness and greediness
to minds of selflessness and generosity.

Come into the spirit of sharing consistently
and enjoy the fruits of its flourishment
with all of the Sonship all over the world,
for the sharing of everything freely
without charge or trade is the power
and strength of miracles to one another.

Connected minds in all its loveliness is mind-to-mind,
spirit to spirit all-knowing and giving freely
is the essence of spirit and creation
because God did it first, He now asks
if we will be willing to follow in His holy footsteps
to rise as miracle minded children.

We are free from the act of
separation, greed and selfish deeds.
Be willing and ready to embrace in unification
where we recognize and celebrate
the achievement of connected minds.

Child of light, let's have a holy parade in honor
of the remembrance of generosity
that is honorably complete
through sweet connected minds.

We reunite into the bliss of liberation
where we rise and rejoice in holy and lovely creations.

Holy Spirit, Help Us

Lead us to the divine love and light of Christ.

Holy Spirit, help us to remember
the holy, wholly, wholesomeness mind of Christ
and His caring tender heart of love and light
who loves us with all His might.

Lead us to the divine love and light
to help us remember
that we too love Him
with all our mind, heart and soul.

Bless us that we are passionately and divinely inspired
to walk alongside of Christ to escape
all the ruthless and bitter fight
of pain and sorrow the world offers.

Holy Spirit, help us learn to remember
that you are our teacher, guide and comforter
towards the divine glistening golden altar
of Christ inside.

Lead us to the divine love and light of Christ

I Am That I Am

Where there is Heaven,
that's all there is, for I AM that I AM.

Where there is love,
there is light.

Where there is light,
there is life.

Where there is life,
there is truth.

Where there is truth,
there is hope.

Where there is hope,
there is faith.

Where there is faith,
there is trust.

Where there is trust,
there is no fear.

Where there is no fear,
there are miracles.

Where there are miracles,
there is salvation.

Where there is salvation,
there is redemption.

Where there is redemption,
there is atonement.

Where there is atonement,
there is forgiveness.

Where there is forgiveness,
there is life eternal.

Where there is life eternal,
there is your glistening golden diamond star.

Where there is your glistening golden diamond star,
there is the great I AM.

Where there is the great I AM,
there is Heaven.

Where there is Heaven,
that's all there is, for I AM that I AM.

Clichés

Clichés become clear over time
at a flip of a dime.

His heart was in so much pain.
I arrived just in the *nick of time*
to help sooth his heartache.
His heart will heal
and *only time will tell.*

Episodes of shattered hearts
in a world of bittersweet events
is always only a matter of time.
In worlds of dreams,
it will happen sooner or later
because no one is exempt
from sweet to bitter.
In some cases, it enters slowly
with the speed of light, or even in slow motion.
When episodes enter swiftly,
it is all over quite quickly.
When they enter slowly,
it seems to last for an eternity.
To experience it in slow motion
feels like it's never ending.

Sometimes, it even seems like we *lost track of time*
because we stop paying attention to time
and this is just how it is in a state of dreams.
Through dreadful episodes of dream worlds,
we become frightened but transform to courage
and you become *as brave as a lion.*
This is where we learn to become fearless
as we wander into distressing excursions.

We grow out of ignorance and negligence,
and become *as clever as a fox*
because when we *step out of the box,*
our mind gets unclogged.

At willingness to learn to be divinely clever
means everything in the altar of memory rises.
It can be as old as the hills
but wisdom, understanding and discernment
enters to behold the ancient things that have always been,
for everyone and everything is an old soul or idea
because it has all happened godzillion times before.

However, this also means that
we are all diamonds in the rough
because every one of us has a brilliant future.
Remember, what we experience does not define us.

Eventually, we are all *as fit as a fiddle*
as we unravel the riddles.
Every single one of us rise to be in great shape
when God drapes the royal cape
of love, joy and peace upon our shoulders.
This is where we are under His wing of safety.
One day, we all see this clearly.

Believe it or not,
we become as *meek as a sheep.*
This is not weakness.
It is the quality of humbleness.
There is nothing cliché
about being *frightened to death*
or scared out of our wits.
All is fair in love and war.

But there is no need to go to any extent
to claim the love of another
because we are love.
A happy ending reduces the severity of problems
that are merely wars' obstacles.
All is well that ends well.
Every cloud has a silver lining.
This is where every problem
has something good in them
when we behold *the writing on the wall,*
where it is already clear and understood.
We just temporarily have amnesia
through the duration of time.

Time heals all wounds
and this is what time is for.
Through the passage of time,
pain and sorrow heals.
Willingness to kneel and ask
for sovereignty and salvation is all it takes.
Trust me, God Almighty never forsakes.
Haste makes waste so do not rush through
because we will make mistakes
that bring about the blues.
Take your time through every episode of life
that will inevitably arrive at its appointed time.

Do not cry frightful tears,
it is better to cry happy tears
because in the end, we all live *happily ever after*
and this is no fairy tale.
In other words, when we *read between the lines,*
we know it will truly be all right.

We will *fall head over heels in love* with each other,
abolishing *waking up on the wrong side of the bed.*

Do not be concerned with *the calm before the storm*
for this only means that silence truly is the norm.

It may seem like we are between
the devil and the deep blue sea
but every difficult situation
offers the opportunity to choose to remember
that every challenge and tragedy
are merely lessons to learn by.

Every frightful episode of each day are simply screenplays,
but God is always nearby to lift us unto the sky
to watch the battlefield from above.
The clichés I share with you in this poem,
we dream up to keep our minds sane.
It's okay to use clichés.

In dream worlds, nothing is ever what it seems.

Silver Sparkle in Me

The spirit is fresh, pure and clean.

It is the essence of holiness and sinlessness
in all its godliness and devoutness
of God's glory and my own.
You have never seen anything so lovely
until you behold the majesty of your gorgeous spirit.
The silver sparkle in me is how my spirit glistens,
for I have seen its splendor in the Heavenly scenes.

As I gaze upon the silver sparkle in me
never once did God hand me a Kleenex
for there are no tears to dry up
only a smile from ear to ear
that I could not let go of.
There is no frown upon my brow
only a pleasurable expression without any question
of the reality of the silver sparkle in me
which is pure, clean and fresh
within the holiness in me.

The authenticity of God's utter simplicity
is an atmospheric electricity of pure loveliness
in all its holiness.
I instinctively know it's okay to draw near
and without any fear, I most certainly do.

The silver sparkle in me is the glistening spark in you
where you remember the essence of your glistening spirit.
Just ask the Holy Spirit, because He knows.

A transformation from flesh to spirit
is the true reality of immortality.

Gift of Light

The gift of light is temporarily exiled in a world,
so tainted you think it cannot be renovated.

Light is an energy force
through which you can see,
it is a gift from your Creator
for He is light as are you too.
Darkness is an energy force
through which you are blind,
an idea you made to quench what fear is.

You are not alone in this idea,
for we, the Sonship made fear
and thought we could withstand it alone.
We made darkness and thought we could see in it.
Eventually, we learn it blinds us.
We can escape this by embracing the love and light within
to outshine the fear and darkness that does not become us.

God our Creator who is love and light
can only create around it because He is
the essence of everyone and everything made and created.
This is His nature and all He wishes to know.
He awaits in patience and in peace for every soul
to be willing to learn and remember
that this is His Will and your own.

Be willing to toss the darkness
to let the Holy Spirit spark the light inside
and you will see how bright you can shine
as you combine your light with Christ.

The gift of light is the essence of His sovereignty
and there will always be plenty.
Here, you can listen to the flow
of His glistening golden waterfall,
where its excitement of love and joy greet you.

As you watch the rise of the sunlight,
remember the gift of light that is forever inside of you
and know that it is quite capable
of outshining the sunrise you view
for you are the gift of light
if you so choose His divine love and light.

The gift of light is the atonement He offers on a daily basis.
When He enters, His delightful aroma follows.

Epilogue

The "points of no return" do not exist when we enable ourselves to behold and know the difference between the truth and falsehood of everything seen and unseen. In other words, when we are no longer blind and deaf, we would have reached the essence of why we say, "points of no return". Many believe that once we are gone that's it, there is no returning. But, through spiritual vision we learn what I call, "points of return." No one and nothing ever goes to waste. We are the co-creators of everything seen and unseen and to behold it from a spiritual perspective through quantum leap is beyond anything I could ever explain. Therefore, you will need to experience it to gain the full knowledge and understanding for yourself but you must be willing to seek it through the guidance of the Holy Spirit from within your own thought process. He is the ultimate authority of your memory whereas God is the ultimate authority on quantum leap.

When you are willing to know the truth without blinders or denial, you will enable yourself to see God's *chef-d'oeuvre* of who you truly are. In other words, we are His genius masterpieces and coauthors in every life script that has ever been written as well as the co-creators of everything illusional that has ever been made, since godzillions ago.

However, anything and everything that is merciless does not come from God. But because He permitted us to create the opposite of what He creates, forgiveness, atonement and the end of time becomes inevitable.

This ensures that we will escape the illusional worlds full of false tales in order to return to the real world of Heaven where everything is true.

When the time arrives for you to see and receive your answers, you will be a witness to His tender presence. The overwhelming hunger to spiritually collect the breadcrumbs and be fed more and more and more over a period of time intensifies. The spirit leaps with joy at the truth of God's word and spiritual vision enters remembrance.

May the grace of God's love and light shine upon every aspect of your mind and life during your duration in illusion.

Conclusion

Earth is a beautiful world intertwined with bittersweet episodes where we go through phases of ambivalence, but also confidence. What this simply means is that our thinking is ever so insane and puny, but also sane and grandeur. We are constantly intervening, seeking to save ourselves, each other and the earth. Yet, the sovereignty of salvation is already within us. We are very capable of salvation through Christ Atonement. And as far as the rescue of earth, well she takes care of herself. Earth is an illusion as well as everything else that withers, rust and turns to dust. So it does not matter what we attempt to do to preserve her, she will deplete like everything else in illusion. The evidence of this is all around us in the kingdom of the universe.

Our brilliant scientific minds who study the universe already know what seems like barren worlds are illusion and they make this no secret. They are worlds that either already been utilized from previous times or they might be in the making of a new world. I will not do any research on it, however. It is all in our memory we just have amnesia so we are forgetful to everything we already know. Just as earth has an invisible axis so does our brain. It is our insane and puny thinking that must be adjusted and salvaged. The goal of this edition is to bring to light what you are very capable of remembering. But, it is only through your willingness that your thinking of insanity can be adjusted through God's tender healing and correcting of mind. Everyone has their prewritten appointed time when their willingness to receive is inevitable. And time is what makes it inevitable.

When your time arrives for the axis of mind to be adjusted is when our insane and puny thinking is healed and corrected. It is here when one begins to behold and know it is not the earth that needs to be changed and saved, it is us.

When the time enters to replenish ill and puny thinking, is when the Holy Spirit tenderly begins to turn minds axis from-upside down thinking to right side up thinking. This is where shift begins. In the end, the glistening circle of hope prevails. And the glory is not only God's, but also your own. Why? Because God is not greedy, He shares His glory and royalties. The spirit is plucked from the pit of the dreary circle of fear and darkness and into the safety of His glistening golden bubble of love and light. His miracles are a quantum leap, be willing to receive His offerings. This brings you into the realm of happiness, sanity and freedom ever so swiftly. The time will come when His miracles will happen simultaneously and this is going to be a glorious episode to witness.

We are not all in the same thinking of spirituality, yet. However, we have been arriving nearer to it since time began, slowly and now ever so swiftly. Turning minds invisible axis from horizontal to vertical simultaneously may or may not be in my era because the way we think of swift is not the same as the way God monitors it. However, it does mean sooner than later. Simultaneous can very well spread in my lifetime.

This is a phase of time that will be pleasantly and gloriously bliss for everyone.

End Notes

At first, Lorenza did not remember that she would continue to write so it was never her intent to write a third edition to King of Innocence and Peace, The Guiltlessness In You, A Poetic Truth, second edition. In fact, it was never her intent to even write a book of poetry, let alone, a second and third. Nevertheless, she is an obedient host of Christ.

In the light of atonement, she beholds the release of remembrance as to what she is to write and share forward at this time of her life. Suddenly, she instinctively knows her work had just begun. Despite her desire to be finished with her first and only poetry novel of God's truth, her mind, once again, opened up like a floodgate to permit His words to flow as they may. For her, it has been a fascinating celestial journey learning through her universal teacher.

She is forever so delighted to be His happy student. She has learned so much in regards to, not only herself and humanity, but also the various species of beings, earth, the universe and its galactic communities and of course, Heaven. She finds herself writing poetry, once again, to share the poetic truth of the fundamental questions of blindness. She did not realize how much of God's truth she beholds inside until the words began to flow urging her to bring them to an overflow into the world where spiritual awakening is urgently needed.

Lorenza claims that just because our eyes are open, does not mean we are awake. In other words, when our eyes are open viewing everything through physical sight, we are spiritually blind. She now understands what it means when people have told her in the past that she walks around spiritually blind so long as she continues to view everything through physical sight.

She admits, she too was asleep for a long time and when this echoed in her memory, she was able to clearly see how self-deceptive she had been to herself. His words bring her great satisfaction to know spiritual minds are correct. It saddens her, however, to realize how blind most people are as they journey through illusion. But, she is overjoyed to be spiritually awakened to the fact that many have been spiritually awake through every phase of illusion to the true reality of God's love and light since the beginning of time. It brings her great joy that she is now part of spiritual minds because this enables her to share God's word forward not only on earth, but also throughout the universes galactic communities and all dimensions.

She remembers from the time she was born, she lived a great part of her life in a war zone in this lifetime. This created a thick dark cloud that followed her everywhere she went. A war zone life was not a pleasant experience. As much as she was constantly attacked, it's a no wonder she made it through. The more she defended herself the deeper she fell into the pit of fear and darkness spiraling further away from who she truly is.

As a child, she found serenity when she climbed to the very top of the leaf-filled tree in front of the house she was raised in. In these moments, she sat up in the tree for hours enjoying the short-lived peace and happiness that came over her like the comfort of a warm veil that blankets her on a cold shivering day or like strong yet gentle arms wrapped around her with such a loving and comforting embrace. One day, as she is up in the leaf-filled tree simmering in the warmth and coziness of peace, she hears a gentle whisper. She shares with you what the gentle whisper says to her in a poem that is in Part 1 – Glistening Roads. The message from the whisper was short lived in a child's memory.

At the time, she did not fully grasp that it was God who spoke to her as a reminder of the love and light inside. The full episode of this part of her life as a child would come into play later when she had her ultimate miracle as an adult, which she elaborates on in another book. As a child, she was so oblivious to His calling, she dismissed His kind words and comfort, and returned to the war zone ready to defeat the attacks on her.

Now that she reflects back on this childhood memory, she sees in crystal clarity the significance of her life script experiences and the encounters with God in that one instant up in the tree. Since her ultimate miracle, she has worked her way out of the thick dark cloud that hovered over her for way too long. At her willingness to know lifted the dense darkness over her enough to be able to see rays of God's light piercing through the now sparse misty cloud. The more she asked to behold His love, light, life and truth, the more the dark cloud dissipates into thin air. Now fully in the light of God, she discerns everything through His divine eyes. She now fully understands, this is the only thing that matters regardless of the ruthless experiences she endured in this lifetime.

She elects to continue to walk in God's love and light and her own to the end of her time on this world in complete and utter humbleness, kindness, patience, peace and faith. Because she values and cherishes that God honored her with the crown of knowledge in time. Her life's goal to the end of her duration on a bittersweet world is to share what God has brought to her memory through His Holy Spirit.

To emerge with God permits her light to shine through, which is a powerful spark that lights up the light of her brethren at willingness to receive it. She asks that you receive it through your own willingness to escape the thick dark cloud that follows you everywhere you go.

Only through Christ Atonement, she enables herself to behold the glorious rays of light probing through the thick cloud until she found herself in the fullness of His light. This is, what she calls, *the great emergent*. This is where she beholds the loveliness of holiness within all the Sonship. This lesson is priceless because it carries her to the splendor of eternal glory where she never defends herself in battle where her destiny is forever in the safety of our Father in Heaven in the trueness of spirit. By agreeing to be born in illusion, she quenched her curiosity to know the craziness of fear and darkness. She has now returned to holy, wholly, wholesomeness, the pureness of true freedom.

Her devotion to God and all the Sonship through the duration of her synthetic life, is to leave a legacy to continue to introduce spiritual vision to all those who are blind and to those who seek to know it. To write God's word on a deeper level of spirituality is indeed majestic! This brings her nothing but joy and peace to have finally reached, as we say, "the point of return," in all its magnitude of holiness and oneness. Now that she gained the remembrance of how to learn the truth about living on a world with a sick and split mind, she can now share it forward. This brings her great joy to be able to do this. She is dedicated to the Holy Spirit Who is her teacher, guide and comforter through illusion and out of this world at the appointed time she rises to return to Heaven where she now knows she belongs. She is looking forward to knowing the greater plan God has for her when she finally reenters Heaven after being gone since godzillions ago.

She does not even ask or try to imagine what miraculous and magnificent deeds God has waiting for her in Heaven, because she knows whatever it is, it is going to be ever so divinely and majestically delightful. It does not matter what tragedies she is assigned to lead someone out of it.

The delightfulness of it is that she is forever working for God continuing to help bring His holy children back home to the safety of His bosom where we all belong. She can't wait for the day that the dream of all worlds are finally over and we can all relax and enjoy each other in holiness and union enjoying the peacefulness of true freedom. She looks forward to returning to create in beautification lavishing in our royalties. Through the spiritual vision of whole mindedness, she can see it is going to be majestically extraordinary!

About The Author

Lorenza Palomino began writing poetry from an early age. At first, she wrote darker pieces until she experienced her own personal miracle on October 22, 2001. Since then, the Holy Spirit has been teaching her how to write about love and light from a much more deeper and meaningful spiritual level. Having understood the nature of spirituality and how to apply it in reality, she now realizes that this was and has been the most important task she was given to learn.

To apply it to herself, humanity, all life forms on earth, the universe, galactic communities and all dimensions has been a special gift that
she wants others to experience as well through her writing.

She has published two books, is working on publishing the third and is simultaneously polishing up other completed manuscripts.
She currently resides in California.

"There is a sense of holy energy residing in all life forms, no matter where you are in the vast cosmic of all creation."

*Scan the QR code to follow Lorenza Palomino on **Instagram***

She's also available on the following social media platforms:

@godzillionloveandlight
Twitter | **Goodreads** | **Amazon** | **Ink Gladiators Press**
Email: **dancingonglisteningwaters@gmail.com**

Author's Recommendations

I highly recommend you read ACIM. Read and study it from the very beginning and at the pace with which you can endure. ACIM can be very overpowering because of the unveiling of the reality of one truth and one falsehood. I highly suggest you pray and invite the Holy Spirit to guide you through the course before you open the book to read and study it.

Ask Him to bless you so you can be a *happy learner* in what you are about to realize as the true reality from within and the false reality that is not of you begins to shift. Always remember, He will always provide you with the answers to all your questions but they might not come as swiftly as you would like. In humbleness, faith and peace, be patient for His reply. He consults with God for every question you ask of Him before He returns with the answer. This is where patience becomes a virtue.

Ask Him to bless you with patience as you move forward with Him. He is the best teacher you will ever have. He is loving, gentle, humble and patient and God asks that we give Him the same respect. He becomes your best friend as you persevere in working closely with Him as He lovingly, gently and humbly unveils the reality of the true world and the reality of the false world.

When guilt and shame attempts to consume you, remember, that He does not look upon what you think you are but lovingly beholds God's *chef-d'oeuvre* in who you truly are. He beholds and upholds the holiness, sinlessness and peacefulness of your sweet delightful spirit and dismisses everything you think you are but that He knows is untrue.

You are God's children of love and light and His ultimate goal is to ensure you are successful in your journey of spiritual awakening to who you truly are and where the Kingdom of Heaven is as it lovingly and patiently awaits your return home. Earth is the kingdom where you learn to awaken to the love and light already in you and when you behold it, you will want to share it with everyone.

Here, you will see that we are all equal and special in the eyes and heart of God. No matter how deep in the pit of darkness you might be, God always achieves His goal in bringing you out of it because this is what He and you willed before you were born into it. Be happy that He has kept His promise to you and brings you out of what you are not, for fear and darkness is unworthy, but love and light is worthy.

You are His masterpiece that God adores and truly loves because you are His creation. He lifts the sweetness of your soul up to His Throne in the true Kingdom of where you are from. You are royalty and truly loved no matter how you think or feel about yourself. It does not matter what you think, say or do that will bring you and others to the brink of insane pain and sorrow. You have the power invested within you to release the burdens of negative forces, releasing the shackles of your own agonies of guilt and shame but you must be willing to surrender your own burdens and those of others to God wholeheartedly which gives you the power to be free through Him.

I pray you remember that all negative forces are not of God. I pray that through the guidance of the Holy Spirit you learn to dismiss them just as He does because He knows they are not real, therefore, they are not of you.

The phrase, *dancing with the devil* is the same as dancing with the ego because the ego is the devil. We just forgot we named it *ego*. Be willing to forgive the very thing you made to be born to worship for a little while and let it go. This is what time is for to learn and remember you must not fear it because fear is what it rises on.

Let your divine power kick in and humble yourself within. Lift the temptation of dancing with the ego at God's golden feet and walk away in faith and peace. You will enable yourself to be a witness to God's divine miracles, for He is the one who brings deliverance from the chains and shackles of the ego's sinister prison. Through the power of God's love and light and your own, you have the strength to turn away from the temptations of dancing with the ego.

Your love and light combined in Christ outshines the beast inside, enabling you to remember the divinity in you. You will remember you were birthed into a world of time to know what it's like to worship a wrathful and puny god with a loud mouth because you have only ever known the loving and tender Father in Heaven whom you have always loved and worshipped.

This is why we are all born to dance with the ego
and for a little while we do, until the time enters
to return to the dance with eternal divinity.

Acknowledgements

I give my humble gratefulness and thankfulness to God Almighty for permitting His Holy Spirit to teach and guide me through quantum leap. Thank you for never taking away what You have already given at creation to ensure we all escape illusion. I am ever so grateful to your miracles.

To Jesus Christ, Lord, savior and brother. Thank you for draping the cape of royalty and peace over my shoulders during the times I could no longer cope with what has been shown to me. I value and cherish Your majestic peace for all eternity.

To my eternal holy friend the Holy Spirit, I am ever so honored to work alongside of you. Thank you for teaching and guiding me to the golden road of Heaven. In humbleness, I bow before your presence in gratitude to your royal comfort and tender ease of taking me through quantum leap. This enables me to behold all that God wants me know.

To my lovely friend Irene Peralez, I give my deepest gratitude to you as my mentor alongside of Christ during the time I am a baby in Him. Thank you for your divine ethereal guidance during the years I knew nothing of celestial righteousness. I value and cherish your friendship forevermore.

I dedicate this book to humanity and all life forms on earth, throughout the whole wide universe, its galactic societies and dimensions. I hope you one day read this book and its series, and are willing to embrace it under the shroud of Christ love and light and that we encircle in love, joy and peace."

Tell Us What You Think

Write to us at **contact@inkgladiatorspress.com**.
We might add your comments on our website as well as feature your Instagram profile.

We appreciate your love for reading.
Thank you!

We remain at your service,
Reena Doss | Founder
Ink Gladiators Press®

www.ingramcontent.com/pod-product-compliance
Ingram Content Group UK Ltd.
Pitfield, Milton Keynes, MK11 3LW, UK
UKHW021346190726
13845UKWH00027B/740

9 788194 941842